978 1258596866

THE
EXECUTIVE
OVERSEAS

THE EXECUTIVE OVERSEAS

Administrative Attitudes and Relationships in a Foreign Culture

John Fayerweather

SYRACUSE UNIVERSITY PRESS

Library of Congress Catalog Card Number: 59–11259

© 1959, SYRACUSE UNIVERSITY PRESS

Fictitious names are used
for all executives and companies in this book.

TO MY MOTHER

Because of whom I write

Acknowledgments

Back of this book stand the time, advice, and help of many people to whom I am deeply grateful.

One group, without whose cooperation the research would have been impossible, must remain anonymous but each of them will know my personal debt to him. I refer to those executives who gave of their time and innermost thoughts that I might understand the problems of administration through their eyes. To them and to their companies I wish to express not only my appreciation, but also my sincere respect, for their willingness to give so generously for the advancement of knowledge and understanding.

Another group is too numerous for individual acknowledgment. Many of my former associates at Harvard Business School stimulated my thinking. I owe a particular debt to the human relations group there upon whose basic research concepts I built in making this study. I am especially grateful to Professors George Lombard and Raymond Bauer who read the full manuscript and made many valuable criticisms and constructive observations.

Along the road many others have provided stimulating comments. I think particularly of Professor Frederick Harbison of Princeton University whose viewpoints helped me to steer the book into an effective pattern and Deans Harlan Cleveland and William Travers Jerome, III, at Syracuse University whose suggestions contributed greatly to the final editing of the manuscript.

Administratively, I am indebted to two men whose efforts have brought the book into being. Dean Stanley F. Teele of the Harvard

Acknowledgments

Graduate School of Business Administration saw the importance of this study and through his efforts the time and money to support the research were provided by the school's Division of Research. Dean Harlan Cleveland of the Maxwell Graduate School of Citizenship and Public Affairs at Syracuse University was instrumental in bringing the book to press. Having traveled the same intellectual road with his associates in the Maxwell School study of overseas operations, he saw the meaning of the book as a working partner of *The Art of Overseasmanship*.

I would also like to thank Mrs. Nancy Carpenter who not only typed endless pages of manuscript, but performed numerous other helpful tasks essential to the completion of the book.

Finally and most of all, I want to acknowledge the great contributions of my wife, Ruth, to this effort. As cook, homemaker and companion, she performed superbly all the roles which our culture requires of a wife. But beyond that, she made major working contributions in transcribing all of my notes in Mexico and analyzing every phase of the study with me. Her willingness to discuss the research for hours on end and review the manuscript over and over again contributed immeasurably to the final product.

While the ideas of many people have found their way into these pages, the responsibility for the contents of the book are, of course, my own.

New York, N.Y.
July, 1959

JOHN FAYERWEATHER
Associate Professor of International Business
Columbia University

Contents

ix

Chapter 1

The Problem

What a way to begin a day! Harry Grey could feel his stomach churning as he listened to Pedro Gomez, the chief purchasing agent.

"Yes, Mr. Grey, we should do something about that parts situation. You see I've been very busy with locating a supplier for the new boxes and Mr. Alonzo has been tied up with the union negotiations. But you can be sure we will get after the parts problem very soon."

The words were different but not the meaning. Harry had heard the same story four times in the last three weeks and there had been other incidents like it that had him pretty well fed up. He had been sent to Mexico nine months ago to get the Farley Company's subsidiary operating on a stronger basis. He'd made headway, but on some problems like this parts situation he seemed to be blocked by his own organization.

Ramex, one of Farley's largest Mexican suppliers, was erratic in meeting delivery dates and the quality of the parts was often below specifications. Raul Alonzo, the production manager, complained about the situation frequently. When Harry had asked him if inventories could be cut so the company could reduce its bank loan, Raul had insisted that he needed that much inventory as long as the supplier was unreliable.

Harry was sure the problem could be solved. There were other suppliers beside Ramex. The obvious approach was for Pedro and Raul to get together and work out a satisfactory procurement scheduling system. Then Pedro should take a firm stand with Ramex and, if

1

they didn't meet his requirements, get a new supplier. He knew this posed some problem for Pedro because the Ramex sales manager was his friend. But the managers of other United States subsidiaries had assured him that it was possible to get good deliveries. Furthermore, Pedro himself had agreed that he could and should do something about the supplier. But for all his agreeing nothing happened and Harry began to feel that Pedro never would do anything about it. He had thought about threatening to fire him, but that didn't make sense. Pedro was an able man and the greater part of his work he did competently. So he restrained the feelings that threatened to stir up his ulcer and tried again.

"Pedro, I don't think you really understand the importance of this problem. If we could get good parts deliveries, we could cut our inventory by 300,000 pesos and reduce our bank loan that much. At 12 per cent per year that would mean 36,000 pesos more profit for the company, a part of it going to you and me in bigger bonuses. I know you have a lot of things to do, but so do we all. This is an important matter and you should give it a high priority. Frankly, Pedro, it doesn't seem to me that you've got your heart in this. If you don't agree with my idea I sure wish you'd say so."

"Oh, I agree with you completely, Mr. Grey. There is no excuse for these poor deliveries and we should straighten the problem out. I'd certainly like to have a bigger bonus, you can be sure of that. I'll get together with Mr. Alonzo right away."

Pedro was trying to handle this thing the best way he could. He liked Mr. Grey and he wasn't at all happy about the way things had been going for the past few weeks. It was natural for Mr. Grey to want to cut costs, but he didn't understand the procurement situation in Mexico. When he had first talked to Pedro about the parts problem, Pedro had tried to explain that Ramex was their best choice as a supplier because they could always be relied on to meet the company's demands. His friend Carlos had never failed him.

It was true that they were sometimes a little late or the parts were not quite up to specifications, but blaming the high inventories on that was ridiculous. That was just like Alonzo. A little variation in the specifications would not hurt production and besides, the production lines were set up so they could switch from one product to another very easily if they did not have just what they needed for a couple of days. Alonzo liked to have a warehouse full of inventory and it was just like him to blame it on procurement. It certainly wouldn't do any good for him to get together with Alonzo and try to work the problem out. There was no use in trying to explain that to Mr. Grey, however, when he didn't even understand about Carlos being so reliable. The best he could do was to keep the situation under control and hope that the boss would eventually see it his way or things would straighten themselves out some other way.

John Macy lay on his bed and watched the fan go around. He felt whipped and he didn't know what to do next. All week he had been working on Vishnu Rama and he had no more effect on him than the fan was having on the heat of Calcutta.

Three years ago the Shave-All Company, of which John was Far Eastern manager, had had a good business exporting razors and blades to India. Then in the face of possible import restrictions the company had turned over its business to a new company financed by the Rama family. The Ramas were leading Indian industrialists who had built a fortune on the production of steel products like picks and shovels and were then interested in expanding to new fields. Shave-All received a minority interest in the new business in return for its trade name and technical aid.

The contract with the Ramas had also specified that they would "actively promote Shave-All products." John thought that it was clearly understood that this meant continuing the aggressive promotion which had been used in India to build the company's sales after World War II from nothing to a high level. Under Rama management, however, Shave-All sales had dropped steadily. It was soon evident that the Ramas were not pushing sales, and in visits and correspondence the company applied increasing pressure for more activity.

When nothing happened, John finally decided he would go to India and stay until he could find a way to get the Ramas moving. That was six weeks ago. He had spent the first month out in the field. He found Shave-All products were being sold from Rama warehouses with virtually no sales effort and that promotion was limited to a few newspaper advertisements and a scattering of posters distributed by the company's ten salesmen. This selling activity fell far short of

Shave-All's former program and that of its leading United States competitor. John then worked up a detailed program designed to re-establish Shave-All's market position.

For the past week he had been trying to convince Vishnu Rama, the sixty-year-old head of the family, that the program should be adopted. But he had argued in vain. John had pointed to the low sales volume and to the Ramas' limited program which he asserted did not meet the agreement. He had supported his proposals in the greatest detail, arguing particularly that Shave-All's previous success and the present results achieved by their competitor proved that strong promotion was worthwhile.

Mr. Rama had expressed appreciation for his interest and efforts, but had agreed to nothing. He observed that a sales drop was inevitable with the change to Indian manufacture. Though sales were lower, the company was making a reasonable profit. He said that to fulfill the contract terms he had undertaken newspaper advertising even though he did not believe in it and its blatant character reflected on the prestige of the Rama family name. A good product was its own best advertisement and on that basis his family had built a great business. He felt that Shave-All had expanded its sales in a special situation right after the war and there was no proof that its promotion program had been essential to that success. Likewise he observed that the United States competitor sold a higher quality blade than Shave-All and it was quite probable that this, rather than the promotion, accounted for their success. In any case, several British concerns in related fields did very little advertising and, since they had been in India for many years, he felt their approach to the market was probably sounder.

John found it hard to meet these arguments. He was sure he was right and equally sure that Mr. Rama was a very competent business-man who should be able to see the logic of his proposals. He had great respect and liking for Mr. Rama and he believed that once he grasped the value of promotion he would do great things for Shave-All in India. But how could he convince him?

Vishnu Rama settled himself to relax before the evening meal and reflected for a moment on the events of the past week. He had spent a great deal of time with the boy from the United States. He was a good boy, full of energy and ideas. He wished he could do something to help him. He drove so hard, and for what? This whole arrangement with the Shave-All Company had turned out rather differently from what the Ramas had expected. The product was good and, left to themselves, his family could develop it into a good business as they had with the rest of their operations.

But they were not left to themselves. Instead there had been constant pushing and arguing. These people from the United States never seemed to be satisfied with anything. Now they had sent out this young man who scarcely knew India to tell the Ramas how to run their business. It was not pleasant at all. He hoped the young man would give up soon.

The stories of Harry Grey and John Macy are distressing but they are by no means unusual. Such incidents are common to the experience of the more than 25,000 United States executives stationed overseas,[1] and the many other home-based United States businessmen who have working relationships with foreign executives. That they should occur is not surprising. Difficulties in the relations between businessmen of different nations have been reported at least since the time of Marco Polo. Today, however, these problems have assumed a new significance because of the great expansion of United States business interests abroad and because of the role which businessmen play in fostering or hindering the growth of amicable relations between nations.

It is with these thoughts in mind that a study of relationships between United States and foreign executives was undertaken. The study was divided into two parts: first, an extensive survey of opinions about administrative relationships in many countries; and second, intensive observation of selected managerial groups in Mexico.[2] The study by no means exhausted all facets of the subject, but it did make substantial progress in revealing the character of the problems which

---

[1] Estimates of United States business personnel abroad vary considerably. The 25,000 figure is a conservative estimate derived from a census of United States companies made by the Maxwell School at Syracuse University. Harlan Cleveland and Gerard J. Mangone, *The Art of Overseasmanship* (Syracuse, N.Y.: Syracuse University Press, 1957), p. 20.

[2] A more detailed description of the research is given in Appendix A.

underlie the difficulties between executives abroad and the approaches which seem to ameliorate the difficulties. Its findings are reported in the pages which follow in the belief that they will help operating executives to achieve more satisfactory relations with their foreign associates.

THE PROBLEM OF CULTURAL DIFFERENCES

One central theme emerged from this research. It is that the significant difficulties in relations between United States and foreign executives are due to the differences in their national cultures. Most of the book will be devoted to elaborating this theme. As a brief introduction to it, we may take another look at the two stories related at the beginning of the chapter.

Harry Grey's difficulties with Pedro Gomez and John Macy's dispute with Vishnu Rama may be viewed simply as disagreements between men with different opinions about how to deal with a situation. Differences of this nature are common in business anywhere and many of the problems of United States executives abroad go no deeper than that. In fact, it is quite clear that there is something more fundamental than a simple difference of opinion behind these disputes. While they are talking about immediate problems, their disagreement concerns basic business concepts of which these problems are just symptoms. Harry Grey believes in buying from suppliers who adhere to rigorous performance standards; he believes department heads should meet problems by collective action; and he believes in direct and open communication between subordinate and superior. Pedro Gomez believes in buying from suppliers with whom he has close personal ties; he believes that procurement problems can be handled best by one man with a minimum of complicating relationships with other department heads; and he believes that it is better to avoid open disagreement with his superiors. Around the world in India, John Macy is expressing his faith in the value and possibility of expanding demand by the active pressures of advertising. His arguments fall on barren ground because Vishnu Rama has relatively little interest in expanding sales aggressively and neither faith in nor respect for advertising.

Differences in business concepts pose the question: "What will work best under existing conditions?" To answer the question, facts must be acquired and analyzed, and disagreements often occur because of inadequacies in this process. The personalized business alliance advocated by Pedro Gomez is traditional in Mexico. A large portion of business is done that way, and Pedro may be right in believing that it is the most effective system. Harry Grey, however, has made a survey of other companies and believes there is factual support for his position. There is an evolution in business relationships under way in Mexico and he also may be right. A similar issue, that of effectiveness of advertising in India, concerns John Macy and Vishnu Rama. In both of these cases, it is obvious that getting enough facts for a definitive answer is difficult and probably not practical within the limits of time and expense which the companies can afford.

Many difficulties in relations with executives of other nations can be reduced essentially to this type of problem. Lacking data, they rely on their feel for the situation and arrive at different conclusions. The area of disagreement in these cases may be reduced if more facts are obtained, and frequently United States executives fall short in this respect. It is a difficult and time-consuming process to learn how the various phases of a foreign business system work and how they interact as an effectively functioning whole. Under pressure to get a job done, the United States executive overseas acts before he has full knowledge of the local system. Likewise, the foreign executive frequently is not alert to the ways the system is changing and the possibility that new methods will work and perhaps work better than the old ones.

Many disagreements can be dispelled or at least reduced in magnitude by bringing in knowledge which is reasonably accessible. But observing experiences like those of Harry Grey and John Macy, one can see that the most difficult portion of the problems cannot be dealt with on a factual, analytical level. Behind these problems is a still deeper level of disagreement.

This deeper level is the level of cultural difference; the level of attitudes, values and objectives which make up a man's personality.[3]

---

[3] The word "culture" in the broadest sense includes all of the attributes of a society: tools, houses, business systems, attitudes, and so forth. In this study, however, the word is used only to mean the attitudes, beliefs, and values of a society. The term "cultural attitudes" might be more proper, but culture alone is simpler and, being quite commonly understood in this usage, it has been adopted. Many of the other aspects of a culture will be referred to as composing the "environment" within which business operates. The borderline between "culture" and "environment" in these two usages is not precise but they provide a practical way of distinguishing between mental-attitudinal forces and physical-structural conditions. The relationship between culture and personality is described in Appendix A.

These forces are constantly at work influencing the conclusions men draw from what facts they have, the assumptions they make when they do not have facts, and most important, the way in which they act. The most significant problems between United States and foreign executives appear to be those in which culturally-based characteristics of this level come into conflict. That is true of John Macy and Harry Grey who have taken positions which strike to the heart of the fundamental codes by which Pedro Gomez and Vishnu Rama live.

Harry Grey, drawing on his own code, proposes that his Mexican associate substitute impersonal, contractual arrangements for the personalized alliances which he has relied on all his life; he asks him to give up some of his independence of action in favor of a life of consulting and compromising with other men in whom he has no faith; and, having made these deeply disturbing demands, he then expects Pedro to change his whole approach to dealing with superiors by stating exactly what he thinks and intends to do.

For his part, John Macy is asking Vishnu Rama to forsake a life of gradual and well-considered advancement in which an honored family name is a prime objective, and to risk both his money and good name in an uncertain venture in which he can see no merit.

Whether the men see the problems in these terms is doubtful. Few executives do. When they work with men who wear the same clothes they do, live in the same business world, speak the same business jargon and in other physical ways appear similar to them, it is hard to realize how deeply their personalities may differ. This is particularly true of those many executives, both United States and foreign, whose knowledge of the character of other countries is superficial—being limited primarily to the business world and having no deep familiarity with family life, religious philosophy and other basic forces.

Lacking an understanding of the true character of their problems, Harry Grey and John Macy pursue their aims with a combination of logic, persistence, and forcefulness. One or more of these ingredients may be enough to accomplish their immediate ends, but whether they will cause any basic change in the attitudes of their associates or establish effective relationships over the long run seems doubtful. It seems more likely that the relationships of these men will be forever bedeviled by disputes until they find some way to adjust to each other in terms of their cultural characteristics.

Here then is the heart of the problem to which our attention must be directed. If we are to find ways to improve relations between United States and foreign executives, we must explore this area of cultural characteristics which contains the seeds of recurring disagreements.

This focus does not ignore the value of increased knowledge of foreign business systems and the environment within which they function. As the comments above indicate, United States executives can improve the effectiveness of both their business decisions and their relations with executives of other nations as they learn more of the facts of the business world in which they work. There are indications that United States business overseas has frequently been inept in its adaptation to foreign business methods, missing opportunities to utilize local institutions and unwisely introducing United States methods. Furthermore, the existing environment is a strong influence on the formation of a culture and thus, as we shall see as the book proceeds, it is an inseparable part of the analysis of the forces which influence the nature of men's personalities.

But the problem of learning about foreign environmental conditions is of a different order from the problem of differences in cultural characteristics, and within the limits of one study it seems important to concentrate on this one basic problem.

AN APPROACH TO UNDERSTANDING

Focusing on cultural differences in relations between United States and foreign executives gives us a starting point. The next question is, "What can we do about it?" It is clearly no problem to be resolved merely by astute thinking and clever use of computing machines. If progress is to be made, it must be made in the basic attitudes and actions of men as they work together and, men of all nations being relatively fixed in their ways, progress will not come easily. So at the outset we need a realistic objective.

Many United States executives have been relatively successful in working with foreign associates. The qualities common to their approaches provide a target for others. In essence these men meet situations by modifying their expectations and actions to the extent which seems necessary to achieve results over both the short and the long term. This modification is frequently instinctive rather than a matter of conscious planning. With some, perhaps, it came naturally; with others it apparently was the result of slow evolution of skill. For a few the modification has gone so far that they have largely lost their initial attitudes, i.e., "they have gone native." It does not appear, however, that the men who have gone that far are in an over-all sense the most effective executives overseas. They are inclined to lose sight of company objectives and to have difficulties in relations with other United States executives and with the home office. The effective men seem to be those who have retained their own attitudes and values intact, but are able to depart from their dictates sufficiently to take positions in relations with foreign executives which are realistic in that they are capable of producing useful results.

The type of action which this point of view calls for is different in every case. For example, we may consider again the stories at the beginning of the chapter. Harry Grey might get the facts from Pedro Gomez and Raul Alonzo and then direct whatever action seemed advisable. Or he might get Mr. Gomez and Mr. Alonzo together and force them to work out the problem themselves. John Macy might propose to Vishnu Rama that Shave-All finance a promotion campaign over several years on the theory that a solid demonstration of its value would convert Mr. Rama. Or perhaps he should just give up, figuring that the company made a mistake in choosing the Ramas, but that after all they are responsible people and left to themselves they will work out a solution. In time they might even pick up a few ideas from Shave-All. The decision in each case depends on a host of business considerations about which we do not know, so that we cannot arrive at a sound conclusion. However, we can observe that as things stand in each case the United States executive is failing in that he is neither getting results nor establishing good relations with the foreign executive for future work, and both of these failures are due to his setting his sights beyond the realistic capacities of the situation.

Avoiding these pitfalls requires three things of a man: (1) understanding his own position—his objectives, his expectations and the effect of his actions on others; (2) understanding the point of view of the foreign executive; and (3) enough flexibility and self-discipline to modify the first to fit the second.

THE PLAN OF THE BOOK

Taking the achievement of understanding as the primary objective, the heart of this book lies in the methodology it presents, a pattern of analysis of a country, its history, its people, their social life, and the effect of all of these things on the administrative attitudes of working executives. The greater part of the book is devoted to elaboration of this framework through extensive application to Mexican management situations, other cultures being mentioned from time to time for illustrative and comparative purposes.

In the analysis the range of attitudes and problems involved in relations between United States and foreign executives are grouped into five main areas with a chapter devoted to each area.

The first three areas are different phases of administrative work. Chapter Two considers the working relationships between men in an organization, that is, how they feel about other men and how they act in work with them. Chapter Three discusses the way in which a man approaches work which is essentially his own, work in which performance depends primarily on his own effort and not his relationships with others. The main elements in this phase are his attitudes toward innovation, analysis, and action. Chapter Four looks behind these attitudes at the motivations of executives, at the nature of their objectives in life and the energy with which they pursue them. In combination an understanding of the way an executive feels in these phases of administrative work gives the United States executive a basis for carrying out his immediate tasks.

But the picture in that form is essentially static and therefore incomplete. The attitudes of many foreign executives are changing and this process may be encouraged or discouraged by the actions of United States executives. So an essential ingredient of his understanding must be a grasp of what is happening to the individual when his attitudes change. Chapter Five is devoted to this topic.

Finally, there are problems of a special nature which arise because of a combination of cultural and nationality differences. In Chapter Six the main problems of this nature are discussed, the ways in which foreign executives may feel about executives because they are from the United States and the impact on them of various approaches which appear to ameliorate the negative side of those feelings.

Chapter 2

Executive Relationships

Men working with men form the substance of the administrative process. The executive in his relationships with his superiors, with his subordinates, with staff men, and with other executives, gives life and meaning to an otherwise chaotic collection of individuals. The ways in which executives work with others are therefore of great importance in the effective functioning of a company.

For executives overseas, these simple truths underlie a tremendous number of problems. Throughout most of the world the cultural attitudes which mold the relationships between men are different from those of the United States. Furthermore, attitudes on interpersonal relations are among the most deeply rooted elements of an individual's personality pattern. He learns them early and they become such a vital part of his life by constant use and reinforcement that they resist change strongly.

It is not surprising, therefore, that a great many of the difficulties between United States and foreign executives observed in this study involved the attitudes of the men towards the conduct of administrative relationships. Approaching situations with expectations born of their own culture, United States executives were repeatedly frustrated, disappointed and confused by the actions of foreign executives. The foreign executives for their part experienced similar emotions as they found their instinctive attitudes did not meet fully the demands of the administrative situations which confronted them. It was clear from observing these problems and from a study of the more satisfactory relationships between United States and foreign executives that an understanding of the way men looked at their relations with others was essential to the establishment of satisfactory administrative processes in bi-cultural organizations.

RELATIONSHIP ATTITUDES

The starting point for this analysis is the outlook of the executive toward the people around him. How does he feel about himself in relation to them? How does he view their relation to him?

To answer such questions in terms of stark contrasts between cultures is dangerous. Differences are never that clear cut. However, it did appear from this research that the cultural differences were great enough so that they could best be described in terms of two extremes. Figure 1 shows diagrammatically the attitudes of two types of individuals.

On the left is the individualistic type of personality. In his essential relationships this type of person walls himself off as much as possible from those around him. The distinction between essential (e.g., work) and non-essential (e.g., recreational) activities is significant because he may be sociable and communicative in the latter while still isolated and secretive in the former. He is not self-sufficient because that is impossible, but maximum self-sufficiency is his objective. He looks upon those around him as necessary evils. He is distrustful, suspecting them of predatory intentions toward him, and he feels a sense of hostility toward them. In any relationship he is intensely concerned with his own position and not very conscious of the attitudes of others except as he perceives their impact on him. As the size of the circles indicates, he is much more concerned with those above him than those below.

On the right is the group-oriented type of personality. Towards those around him he has a feeling of union. His satisfactions are in considerable measure achieved as group objectives or just in being a part of a team. He views those around him with confidence, sensing that they have the same group objectives as he. He gives only slightly more thought to his superiors than to his subordinates. Brief descriptions of two Mexican executives will make these generalizations more meaningful. Neither of these men fits the stereotype, but their tendencies run strongly in the directions of the two extremes.

Figure 1

ATTITUDES TOWARD OTHER MEN

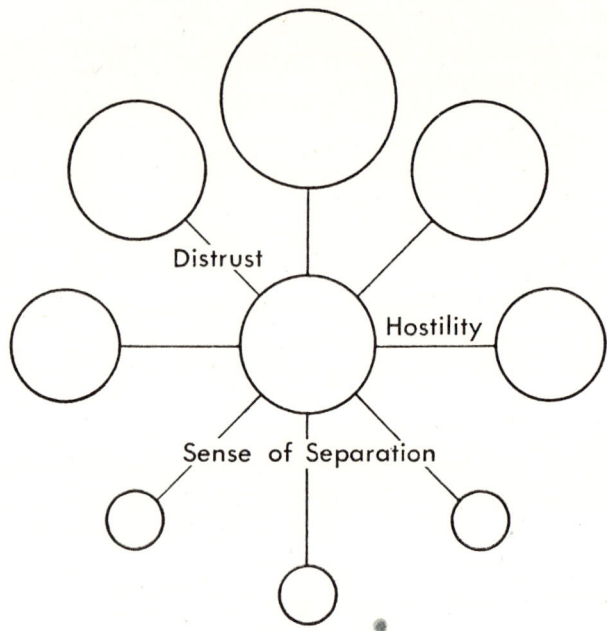

Individualistic Personality

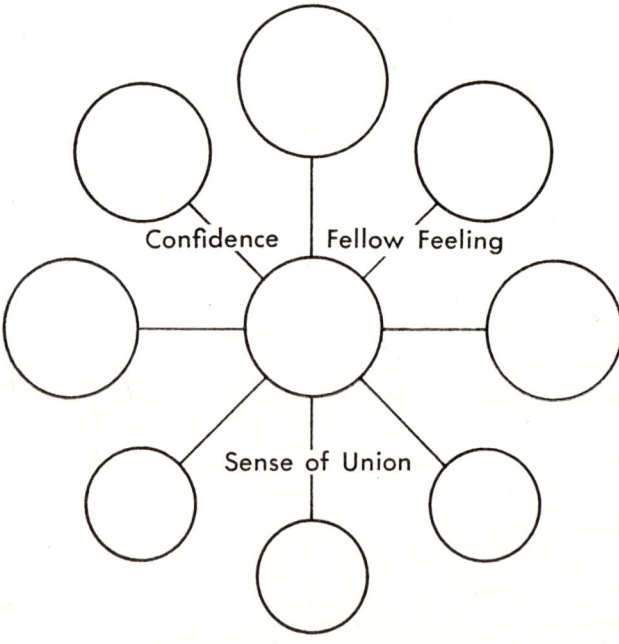

Group-Oriented Personality

Ramon Guzman's thoughts were focused almost entirely on himself and his job, the two being essentially the same in his feelings. He rarely thought about other people except as they impinged on his own work. He had several assistants, but they were not much on his mind. He was capable of forgetting that he had talked to one of them ten minutes after the conversation. The chief exception was a man who had been brought in from another part of the company to handle a new section in his department because Mr. Guzman was overworked. This experience had troubled him deeply because he knew he was overworked and he liked the man; yet in the process he had had to give up a function which he had performed for several years and which had been one of the prime bases for his importance to the company.

His job involved contact with several other departments, but he did not give much thought to their activities. One department was in a better position to get some information which his department needed regularly, but he was scornful of their competence. "It's up to me to get my own information." He was a man of kindly nature and had advanced to a point where further promotion was unlikely. He had little occasion, therefore, to compete, but when a dispute arose with another department, he became a tough and aggressive fighter, reacting at times with great emotion to what he saw as challenges to his position.

In his view, his advancement was attributable to his own competence in learning the techniques of his job. He gave no credit to his superiors, viewing them either as "tough nuts" with whom he had dealt satisfactorily, or nice fellows who knew their jobs and with whom he got along all right. He handled the functions of his department competently and had made some important individual contributions on his own initiative. He doubted, however, if anyone appreciated them. "You just do your best for the company. That's what you're paid for."

Raphael Cordova was another sort of man. He always seemed to be thinking about other people. First it was a man from another country coming to Mexico for training, then one of his own men who was having trouble adjusting to a new job, and then an employee who was sick. His immediate preoccupations were largely with building up the abilities of his staff. He said he wanted to have more time for planning, but watching him visiting around among his associates every day, one sensed that he would always spend a good deal of time thinking about them. To date, he had always known how to do every job better than his assistants, but he had just sent one man to the United States to learn a technique he did not know. He seemed intrigued by the prospect that "When he comes back he'll know more than I do."

Early in his career with the company Mr. Cordova had had a violent battle with the head of another department who had been giving orders to his assistants. He had rather enjoyed this experience and had ended up on good terms with the other man. There had been no further trouble with direct invasions of his territory. His relations with different departments were friendly and he spent a good deal of time in formal and informal talks with the other executives about company problems. He came down very hard on one of his assistants who took an uncooperative attitude toward a staff man.

Mr. Cordova was very happy in his present job because after a couple of unfortunate experiences he had at last found a company where people had confidence in him and gave him a chance to work up to the limit of his capacity. He had found life very satisfying with this group and became quite emotional in talking about some of the experiences they had had, like the time they brought a new product from the drawing board to the market in a month. "We really had to put our whole effort into it, but we did it. We beat our competitor by just a week. That really threw him off."

The differences between the individualistic attitudes typified by Ramon Guzman and the group-oriented attitudes found in Raphael Cordova provide a contrast which is useful in understanding differences in executive attitudes throughout the world. One cannot, of course, compress into one dichotomy the wide range of personality characteristics which people show. Each man's attitudes toward others are a composite of many feelings. As a practical guide to understanding, however, the individualistic-group oriented concept appears useful as it is descriptive of feelings which are observed to be of prime importance in bi-cultural administrative situations.

The individualistic attitudes were those observed most frequently in Mexico and they are apparently common in most of the cultures of the world. The attitudes in India provide another example:

On the job it is somewhat foolhardy to put too much faith in others—superiors, peers, inferiors . . . Some think that superiors grab all the credit for whatever is done by an inferior, that fellow workers have to be watched lest they manipulate to their own advantage, and that subordinates will deceive and shrug off responsibility.[1]

And in Germany:

There were other indications of fearful and suspicious attitudes toward people. The Germans were more worried than the Americans about finding friends who were trustworthy, or who were similar to themselves. In answering a question about what might create a worried, nervous feeling, the Germans were more likely than the Americans to feel nervous and apprehensive about other people.

In the interviews there was some discussion of group situations, and of human relations problems. The German approach to these problems seemed to demand clear structure and strong leadership as a means for avoiding the eruption of interpersonal tension. When asked what might cause difficulty in a group situation, the Germans mentioned difficulties between people, and the Americans mentioned individual resistances. The Germans saw the difficulty provoked by interaction; the Americans, by lack of interaction. If one accepted the German premise, the only way to avoid difficulty was to avoid interaction. Thus structure and restraint as a means of control were considered more appropriate in a small group situation than in any other situation. General problems of democratization and social change could be met through education and individual initiative but small group problems required that strict restraints be placed upon individuals. Opposition should be brought into line, and the right ideas be made to prevail.[2]

In varying strengths, group-oriented personality characteristics were observed in a number of Mexicans covered by the study, but these individuals stood out as exceptions to the general cultural pattern. The group-oriented attitudes are part of the dominant ideology of the current culture of the group from which a large portion of United States executives abroad are drawn. Thus these attitudes generally prevailed in the expectations of United States executives even though their own attitudes showed considerable range, some being relatively individualistic, while most tended toward the group-oriented type.

[1] Ruth Hill Useem and John Useem, "Images of the United States and Britain Held by Foreign-educated Indians," *The Annals* (Philadelphia: The American Academy of Political and Social Science), September, 1954, p. 74.
[2] Jeanne Watson and Ronald Lippitt, *Learning Across Cultures* (Ann Arbor: University of Michigan, 1955), p. 26.

VALUES

The attitudes of an executive toward other people govern the intentions and frame of mind with which he will approach an administrative relationship. To understand the way in which he will actually conduct the relationship we need to explore a second set of attitudes, the man's system of values. Each person has a code to guide him in his actions, helping him to decide what is appropriate and inappropriate in any situation. In large part these codes are incorporated into the culture of a society taking the form of generally approved opinions as to what is "right" or "wrong." More often than not the weight of religious authority will be thrown behind their enforcement.

The power of a culturally supported system of values and the intensity of the individual feelings which usually surround it make it difficult to view the subject objectively. This is especially true for the United States executive who comes from a rigorously moralistic culture. In relationships between United States and foreign executives, such attitudes add unfortunate complications. Whereas an executive may view differences with a foreign executive on attitudes toward other men as "undesirable," he is inclined to pass a much stronger judgment against differences in values as "bad."

The problem for the United States executive is therefore twofold: to understand the nature of differences in value systems and to retain a degree of tolerance in dealing with them. The extent of tolerance which is advisable is hard to gauge because it does appear that there are elements in some foreign systems of values which are undesirable, just as there are shortcomings in the United States system of values. The only conclusion this research could support was that an initial disposition toward objectivity and open-mindedness is essential.

The forms in which the United States executive may encounter differences in value systems are varied and often ill-defined. There is a basic moral code common to practically every civilized nation, whether it be derived from the Judeo-Christian tradition, from Buddhism, Confucianism, Mohammedanism, or some other source. For example, stealing and lying are universally considered bad, and being kind to people and honoring one's parents are considered right.

Systems of values, as the term implies, are concerned with the importance assigned to different elements in the basic code and not with the code itself. The cashier whose mother needs an operation he cannot afford looks to his system of values to tell him whether it is worse to do nothing for his mother or to steal from his employer. There are a tremendous number of individual decisions of this sort which every man must face. His system of values will sometimes give precise answers, but more often it will provide weightings in favor of general principles which will form the basis for action. Thus, in much of the world the respect accorded to the property of employers and the value of honesty in the abstract are so much lower relative to kinship obligations, that the cashier would have little difficulty in deciding to steal. On the other hand, there are some areas where looseness of family ties and the general sanctions of society against stealing are such that the decision would go the other way.

The problem for the United States executive, therefore, is to acquire a feel for the general weightings which foreign systems of values prescribe. In this book it is clearly impossible to convey such a feel. It is possible, however, to outline two basic conflicts in values which are observed to be significant in administrative situations and to convey thereby a sense of the direction in which foreign systems of values may vary from those common to the United States culture. The two basic conflicts are (1) accuracy and directness versus maintenance of satisfactorily controlled relations; and (2) loyalty to a general code of conduct versus pursuit of personal advancement.

One of the commonest complaints of United States executives abroad is that their associates do not talk to them honestly and directly. This problem is often seen as a direct affront to the United States executive or a sign of low moral standards on the part of the foreigner. Those terms, however, do not contribute much to understanding the problem. The story of Harry Grey and Pedro Gomez in Chapter One is a good illustration. Mr. Gomez was not a man of low moral caliber nor was he consciously trying to affront Mr. Grey.

To understand such situations it is necessary to appreciate the system of values which the foreign executive is following as he weighs the merits of frankness against avoiding a dispute with his boss or, in terms of the broader value generalization, the merits of accuracy and directness versus the maintenance of satisfactorily controlled relationships. Mr. Grey and Mr. Gomez differ because they come from cultures whose dictates on this issue are opposed. In the United States culture directness, accuracy, honesty, and frankness are qualities which carry such great ideological approval that in most situations adherence to them is expected to take precedence over other values. Under some circumstances the actions of a United States executive may not conform to this code, but, because it is part of the ideology, he is likely to feel a degree of guilt or dissatisfaction with himself for not living up to the ideal. And it forms the standard for the expectations with which he approaches his relations with others. In Mexico and most other cultures, the maintenance of proper relationships is considered more important. The ideology recognizes that there are many circumstances under which the individual need not, in fact should not, state his own opinions.

These opposing valuations are tied closely to the differences in attitudes toward other men which were just discussed. For the group-oriented personality the free exchange of information is both natural and essential. The sense of union and confidence he has with others in his working relationships can only be based on the assurance that they are informing him of the things which he should know, and to achieve their confidence he must be prepared to share his thoughts with them.

For the individualistic personality on the other hand, there can be no expectation of beneficial reciprocity. Surrounded by individuals in whom he has little trust, his assumption is that any information he gives may be used by others for their advantage at his expense. To him, the important thing, therefore, is to choose wisely what he will and will not tell in order to maintain the relationships with those around him in the most satisfactory manner.

Viewed in this light, the differences in values become more meaningful. Each is the logical corollary of the system of interpersonal attitudes of the culture.

A similar relationship with personality traits is involved in the issue of loyalty to a general code of conduct versus pursuit of personal advancement. In the United States culture great importance is attached to a variety of actions which are considered essential to the good of society. They include "being a good sport," "giving the other fellow a break," and "sticking to the rules of the game." Thus, while the United States culture gives great encouragement to a man in advancing himself, he feels constantly constrained in his efforts to do so by this diffuse code which limits his freedom of action, a code which is enforced by powerful pressures of social approval and disapproval.

The relation of this code to attitudes toward people is again quite logical. Confidence and trust in others must be based on the assumption that their intentions toward the individual are friendly, or at least that they will not harm him. In a society where one has a variety of relationships, assurance of this sort can only be provided by a generally accepted code. Thus, the existence of group-oriented attitudes in a culture goes hand in hand with values which subordinate the advancement of the individual to the preservation of the general code of conduct.

No comparable constraints are necessary in an individualistic type of culture. In fact, "to give the other fellow a break" when you know he will simply use it to push you aside is pure folly. We find in a society like Mexico's many kindly people who are helpful to others, but the culture does not press a man to put such actions ahead of his personal interests. The result is a system closer to fully independent competition and struggle for survival than that which we have in the United States.

These two aspects of systems of values illustrate the types of differences which United States executives may encounter abroad. They have been portrayed quite simply and neatly for the sake of clarity. In reality, they are seldom encountered in such simple form. Probably the reader will have noted to himself United States executives whose systems of values ran counter in some ways to what has been described as the United States cultural pattern. Likewise, in this research Mexicans were observed who, to varying degrees, conformed to this dominant United States pattern. And to make the situation even more confusing, many executives demonstrate a notable ambivalence in their system of values, sometimes showing one attitude and sometimes another.

The differences which have been described do, however, point the way toward the areas of action and thinking in which the systems of values of men from various cultures may differ.

The Roots of Mexican Culture

The way in which systems of values are tied to attitudes toward other people underscores the unified character of cultures. They are in the fullest sense *integrated* sets of beliefs. It is for this reason that a thorough knowledge of the history and life of a country seems to be essential for effective work abroad. An outsider who finds himself deeply involved in the life of a country, whether he be a business executive, a missionary, or an invading military commander, must understand not only the individual idiosyncrasies of the culture but also their relationship to one another. He cannot usually deal effectively with one characteristic without knowing how it relates to others.

To lay a firm foundation for the discussion of the cultural attitudes affecting foreign executives, it will be helpful to step back for a minute to review the type of historical and national forces which mold cultures, using Mexico as a case example. Each country, of course, has a unique history and culture. Mexico serves well as an example, however, not only because it shows the types of forces that help form a culture, but also because there are a number of similarities between it and other countries.

Until 1821 Mexico was a colony ruled by the Spanish king. There was a large, corrupt government bureaucracy. The economy of the country was based on great agricultural haciendas and, to a lesser extent, on silver mines. The Catholic church dominated the people and was rich in land and money. The wealth and power in the country was controlled by the small Spanish population. The masses of Indians were poor and worked in actual or virtual slavery for the Spanish.

In this society, a man's chief opportunity for advancement lay in receiving favors from those above him and exploiting those below. Positions in government were eagerly sought (and bought) because they carried power which could be used to extract bribes from those who wanted land, mineral rights, or other concessions. The owners of haciendas and mines profited largely through the number of Indians they could impress into servitude. Many priests fattened the coffers of the church and their own pockets at the expense of the superstition-ridden natives.

Out of this environment the cultural attitudes of the day were born. A man fought, intrigued, and bargained for a position from which he could exploit others for his own advantage. In large part, the struggle for success was fought in maneuvers under the table and behind the scenes. The essence of the tactics of the day are summed up in the expression which still guides many Mexicans: *Mañas son mas fuerte que fuerza* (tricks are stronger than force). Other men could serve as allies and helpers in the fight, but with the opportunities limited and the competition tough, few men could be really trusted.

Independence from Spain did not change this basic picture. As a leading historian put it, "Independence deteriorated into a struggle for who could get the most personal plunder out of the country."[3] A few high-minded leaders like Benito Juarez flashed across the political horizon, but life in the ranks of the government, the church, the haciendas, and the mines changed very little.

In 1910 the dictatorial president, Porfirio Diaz, was overthrown and since then there have been important changes in the structural elements which molded the Mexican culture. The way in which these changes in the environment are laying the basis for changes in cultural attitudes is discussed in Appendix A. One of the most significant is the rapid rise to importance of the professional management organization required by modern industry. Large organizations existed from the earliest days in the church and government, but they provided little pressure for efficiency. The administrative attitudes of the individualistic personality were accepted and men had wide freedom to utilize their positions for their personal ends.

In the economic sphere virtually all organizations were one man shows ranging from push cart merchants to factories dominated by the owner-manager whose subordinates served only to transmit and enforce his orders. In this system success went to the entrepreneur who could outwit, outmaneuver, and outbargain the others, a game for which the individualistic personality was well-suited. Wherever the trader merchant has dominated economic life, attitudes of the individualistic type are emphasized. William H. Whyte's description of the attitudes in the United States wholesale drug trade which he acquired as a trainee of the Vick Chemical Company in 1940 are illustrative:

> "Fella," he [the supervisor] told me, "you will never sell anybody anything until you learn one simple thing. The man on the other side of the counter is the *enemy*." It was a gladiators' school we were in. Selling may be no less competitive now but in the Vick program, strife was honored far more openly than today's climate would permit. Combat was the ideal—combat with the dealer, combat with the "chiseling competitors," combat with each other. There was talk about "the team" but it was highly abstract. Our success depended entirely on beating our fellow students, and while we got along when we met for occasional sales meetings, the camaraderie was quite extracurricular.

[3] Ernest Gruening, *Mexico and Its Heritage* (New York: Century Company, 1928), p. 51.

Slowly, as our sales-to-calls ratios crept up, we gained rapacity. Somewhere along the line, by accident or skill, each of us finally manipulated a person into doing what we wanted him to do. Innocence was lost. . . . The advice of the old salesman now became invaluable. While he had a distaste for any kind of dealer, with druggists he was implacably combative. He was one of the most decent and kindly men I have ever met, but when he gave us pep talks about this enemy ahead of us, he spoke with great intensity. Some druggists were good fellows, he told us (i.e., successful ones who bought big deals,) but the tough ones were a mean, servile crew; they would insult you, keep you waiting while they pretended to fill prescriptions, lie to you about their inventory, whine at anything less than a 300 per cent mark-up, and switch their customers to chiseling competitors.[4]

The situation of the group of executives who manage a modern industrial unit is essentially different. Their futures are tied to the accomplishment of an organizational aim: the profitable and expanding operation of their company. The individual has a competitive relationship toward others in the company as he seeks to improve himself, but his value to the company is dependent on his ability to limit his competitive actions where necessary for the common good. The common good calls for exchange of ideas, coordinated efforts, and mutual confidence among the executives.

The conflict between these requirements and the individualistic-trader attitudes is increasingly apparent to Mexican executives and it is a strong pressure in the direction of cultural change. Whatever this and the other environmental changes may portend for the future, however, the attitudes formed during the first four hundred years of Mexican history show great persistence in the individualistic personalities and accompanying systems of values which are dominant in Mexico today.

Accounting in part for the persistence of these attitudes are the influences of the great social institutions of the society: the family, the church, and the schools.

The family is doubtless the strongest of the three. Here, in the words of Mr. Ramirez, a Mexican executive, is a vivid picture of the ways in which life in a traditional Mexican family may affect a young man.

---

[4] William H. Whyte, *The Organization Man* (New York: Simon and Schuster, 1956), p. 117.

"The father in the home has full authority. He is essentially an autocrat. The wife is more or less his property. She must be obedient to him. She frequently finds a way out of this position by lying to him or maneuvering around him, but she must give formal obedience.

"The father's relationship with the child is restricted to setting policies and to providing the strong punishment. There is definitely a feeling of fear about the father. The mother will say, 'Wait until your father comes home and he'll punish you for that.' This will create a great trembling in the child.

"The state of dependency of the child is extremely strong. It is difficult for him to break his links with home. It's a very painful process. When he wants to get married, he usually needs the approval of the parents, and this may well not be an economic matter. He may be earning more than his father, but emotionally he needs this approval.

"The father gives orders without there being any discussion. He takes the position that he knows all. There tends to be a state of rebellion on the part of the child. There always comes a point where he asks himself, 'Is my father as powerful and all-wise as I think he is?' When he asks this question he will usually determine that he is not. He will then have to determine whether he will make an actual break with the parent or submit. Submission may take the form of an actual breaking of his spirit or a lying, evasive position. The type of person who is actually broken rarely becomes an executive. The person who takes up the evasion has a strong, individualistic spirit, a strong character, and this type of person may well become an executive.

"There is no possibility that the greater freedom will be given by the parent. The parents have no conscience about emancipation in the same sense that they have in the United States. That is, they have no desire to give freedom. Therefore, if the child is to make a break, he makes it of his own volition. The parent may accept the idea that the child has broken off. This will be done grudgingly, but it may be done so that the lying relationship is not necessary. But this is not particularly common.

"The man has a real conflict in regard to talking to the mother. Every Mexican must be *macho*, must play the role of the *hombre*. On the other hand, he feels insecure. The *macho* tendency keeps him from talking to his mother. He does not want to get involved in anything which may be involved in feminine thinking and he doesn't have a great respect for female opinion. Thus he has a tendency not to ask his mother things. On the other hand, he looks to her with considerable longing and he may submit to this feeling of insecurity and ask his mother's advice about work and similar matters.

"He will talk to his father very little. He will ask him about very important matters, not in a way of seeking advice, but usually will just get a straight opinion or policy decision from the father.

"Essential to this whole thing is a feeling that he takes for granted that he will have to fight in life. That if he does not fight, he will be regarded as womanly. Thus he does not look toward his father or, in fact, anyone else as particularly someone who will be a helper or adviser. Almost everyone is essentially an adversary or potential adversary. For this reason, he will tend to go to his father if he needs strength, but not for advice.

"He will sometimes help his brothers, but on the whole, the relation between brothers is one of competition. The whole attitude toward the brother is, 'Who is better?' They compete for the favor of the parents and the parents will foster the competition, saying to one brother, 'Look, you're not as good as this one here.'

"The attitude of competition is different in the United States than in Mexico. In the United States, it tends to be rather diffused. It is a question of keeping up with the Joneses and in general raising yourself with regard to the whole society. In Mexico, there is a much smaller universe with which one can compete. Just the close friends and family relationships. You don't give a darn about the neighbors. That's another world, but you care intensely whether you have as good a refrigerator as your brother-in-law."

One aspect of the child's training which Mr. Ramirez' remarks only hinted at, plays an important role in a Mexican's conduct. That is what is described as *educacion*, which is quite a different thing from education in the common sense. *Educacion* refers to manners and good conduct and it is regarded as very important in the training of a child. From an early age he is taught to say the right things on each occasion and to conduct himself in a proper manner, especially before his superiors. One result of this training is a side of the personality of many Mexicans which is often very confusing to the United States executive. When he introduces himself, a Mexican will often conclude with *"su servidor"* or, when he gives his address, he may say *"Es su casa."* In very few cases does it turn out that the Mexican intends to be the executive's servant or even that the executive will be a welcome guest in his house. These expressions are simply part of *educacion*, and representative of a whole cultural attitude, an attitude which places greater emphasis on form than on fact.

The importance of *educacion* lies behind one further confusing aspect of the Mexican culture. It is hard for an outsider to see how the absolute authoritarian father can co-exist with the deception characteristic of many wives and children. The answer is that the father is not in many cases concerned with the fact of obedience, but only with the form. As one Mexican puts it, "He is satisfied if his children obey, right or crooked." [5] The same attitude carries over into business. In the words of a United States executive with experience in several Latin countries, "The boss doesn't mind if the assistant doesn't do as he was told because he didn't care much how it should be done in the first place." In some authoritarian societies, this same sort of tolerance does not exist. In Germany, for example, actual obedience is generally demanded by the superior.

One further element in the attitudes of a young Mexican needs elaboration. That is the problem of loyalties and competition among brothers and contemporaries which was touched on in Mr. Ramirez' remarks. The whole attitude toward contemporaries has been confused in the minds of many United States executives by the strength which is attributed to kinship ties, *compadre* relationships, and business friendships. These relationships have been understood to include great personal loyalty and mutual understanding. In fact this does not appear to be an accurate view of many of these relationships. The following quotation provides another perspective on the question.

> In view of the frequent statement by Mexican students that Americans are friendly but their friendships are shallow, Mexican attitudes toward friends are especially interesting. Thirty-seven out of forty-two students responding showed either neutral or marked hostile attitudes toward their friends. Both personal observation and literary sources show the intimate loyal "best friend," *el amigo intimo,* to be very important in Mexico but many students thought such friends to be very rare. [6]

[5] Rogelio Diaz-Guerrero, "Neuroses in the Mexican Family Structure," *Journal of Psychiatry*, December, 1955, p. 415.
[6] Ralph L. Beals and Norman D. Humphrey, *No Frontier to Learning* (Minneapolis: University of Minnesota Press, 1957), p. 42.

It seems more realistic, therefore, to view most of the close relationships which a Mexican establishes as alliances between individuals who derive mutual advantages from close association. In some cases these alliances may be established along traditional lines and the individual participates in them without deliberation. The family unit is the chief example, and the Mexican family is notable for its tightness and internal loyalties. Other alliances are of a temporary nature designed to serve a specific objective in business, politics, or some other area. Among a people who are intensely individualistic and competitive, such alliances are important in providing help and a sense of security for the individual and in stabilizing the society. They do not, however, eliminate the underlying hostility which characterizes Mexican cultural attitudes even in family relationships.

The same type of thinking applies to paternalistic bonds between superior and subordinate. The father or employer demands that the subordinate render dutiful service to him. In return, he accepts a large degree of responsibility for the welfare of the subordinate. Where the superior or *patron* is reasonably responsible and benevolent, the subordinate will feel a strong sense of security in such a relationship and have a real loyalty to the *patron*.

The church and the schools are not as powerful forces as the family, but they have been influential in reinforcing the attitudes formed at home. Both the Mexican priest and the school teacher have traditionally been authoritarian figures—distant in their relations, passing down opinions and judgments without expectation of disagreement from their flocks. A highly individualistic, competitive attitude is encouraged in the educational system. *Educacion* has been emphasized in the schools and, in a slightly different manner, it has been reinforced by the church. Especially in the pre-revolution times, the church in Mexico was more concerned with dogma and ceremony than with the moral aspects of religion. The contrast of cultures on this count is drawn sharply by the Mexican Jose Iturriaga:

Of the three parts into which religion is usually divided, the Mexican is more inclined towards dogma and the scrupulous observance of ceremony than towards morality. This fact is clearly explained if one remembers that the two cultural worlds from which he sprang were distinguished by the preponderant role of a spectacular liturgy and an immovable and hermetic dogma on the Spanish side, and, on the Indian side, by a faithful observance of ritual. In this sense, the difference between Mexicans and

Figure 2
RELATIONSHIPS WITH OTHER MEN

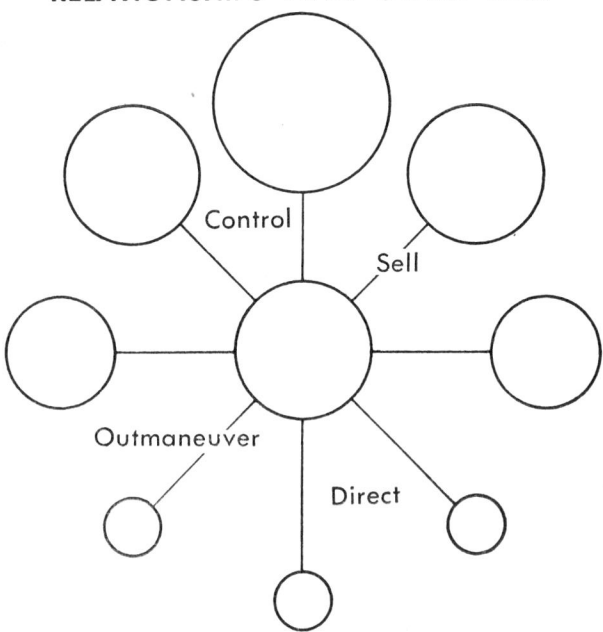

Control

Sell

Outmaneuver

Direct

Individualistic Personality

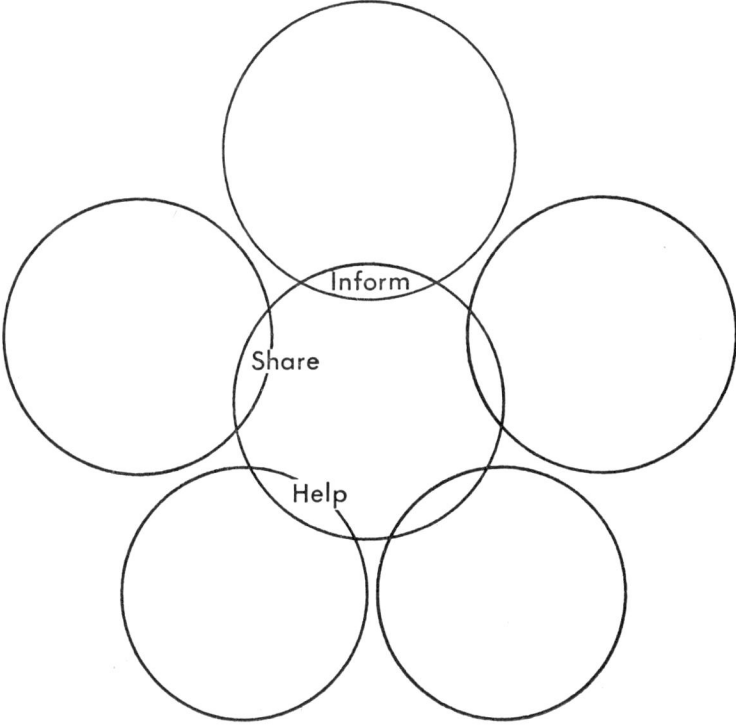

Inform

Share

Help

Group-Oriented Personality

Anglo-Saxons is notable, since the latter prefer morality and social service to ritual and worship, which are almost always poverty-stricken in the Protestant religions.[7]

Thus is formed the individualistic character which fitted well with the traditional Mexican environment. The major influence is the authoritarian father, a figure common to most countries of the world. In other countries, the effects of an authoritarian upbringing at home, in the church, and at school may have somewhat different effects, but the studies of social scientists in varied societies indicate that the results are likely to be much the same. Supplementing these effects is the strict training in correctness of manners, with less concern for correctness in action, also a characteristic of many cultures, notably those of the Orient.

PATTERNS OF ADMINISTRATIVE ACTION

Given their attitudes toward people and their systems of values, how do executives of different cultures act? What type of administrative relations do they establish and how do they conduct them? These are the practical questions the executive overseas faces in adjusting his expectations to the character of his foreign associates. The answers to them are shown roughly in the diagrams in Figure 2.

The individualistic personality at the top works as a separate entity, keeping as much distance as possible administratively between himself and others. Relations with others are conducted in such a manner as to improve his position with a minimum loss of isolation. The words "control," "direct," "maneuver," and "sell" are descriptive of his interactions. These are means for accomplishing a specific aim through a somewhat detached relationship in which the individual retains a large measure of personal independence.

The relationships of Mr. Garcia are representative of this pattern. Mr. Garcia's responsibilities included supervising a number of men and maintaining relationships with his superior and three other department heads. He saw these people almost every day, but his rela-

[7] Jose E. Iturriaga, *La Estructura Social y Cultural de México* (Fondo de Cultura Economica, Mexico, 1951), p. 242.

tions with all of them were distant and carefully controlled. He had an objective and a plan of action for almost every interaction. He avoided situations which he could not readily control. His reaction to informal staff meetings was characteristic, "They go around the room and they ask, 'Do you have anything you want to say? Do you have any problems?' and everybody says, 'No.' That's ridiculous, of course; we all have problems. But you don't want to talk about them there." Occasionally, he would be caught in a situation which got out of control and he would be emotionally upset for several days thereafter. Most of the time, however, he succeeded in accomplishing his objectives by well-planned maneuvers. When a problem arose he would work out a complete solution to it by himself and then either try to get it accepted in full by such maneuvers as the situation required or, if necessary, turn it over to others for them to rework independently.

The relationships of the group-oriented personality at the bottom of Figure 2 are notably different. As indicated by the overlapping circles, his life is constantly interwoven with the lives of the men around him. Intellectually and emotionally he is tied to them. He is always sharing things with others, telling them his problems and discussing theirs. "Informing" and "helping" describe the nature of most of his interactions.

The relationships of Mr. Fuentes followed this pattern. He liked people and they liked him and came to him to talk about their work. In working out problems he consulted with others frequently. The full exchange of ideas was his standard of effective relationships, a point which he expressed with the traditional Mexican vehemence: "There's a new generation of men coming along who have a different philosophy about these things. We get in arguments, and we'll fight like the dickens, but there's nothing personal about it. As soon as the argument's over, we can be friends again. Now, one thing I've always done is to be completely honest. When I see something, I tell a man straight out. I don't believe in this going around under the table and round behind people."

These are the general characteristics of the relationships of the two types of men. To see how they apply in practice, we shall look in detail at the three main types of relationships shown in Figure 3: with superiors, with subordinates, and with nonlinear associates.

Figure 3
ADMINISTRATIVE RELATIONSHIPS AND ATTITUDES

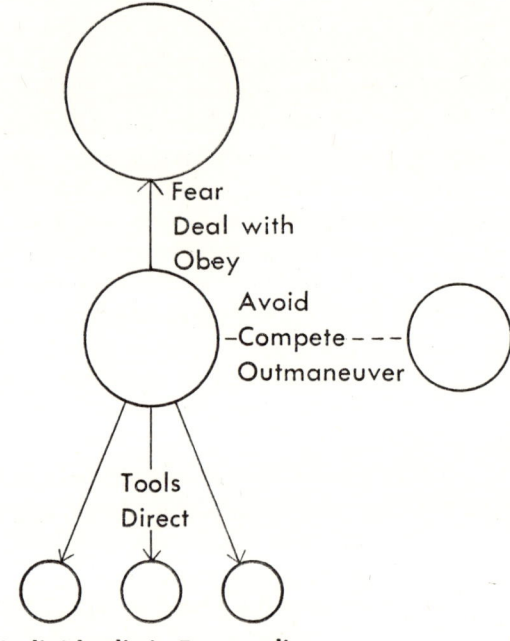

Fear
Deal with
Obey

Avoid
–Compete – – –
Outmaneuver

Tools
Direct

Individualistic Personality

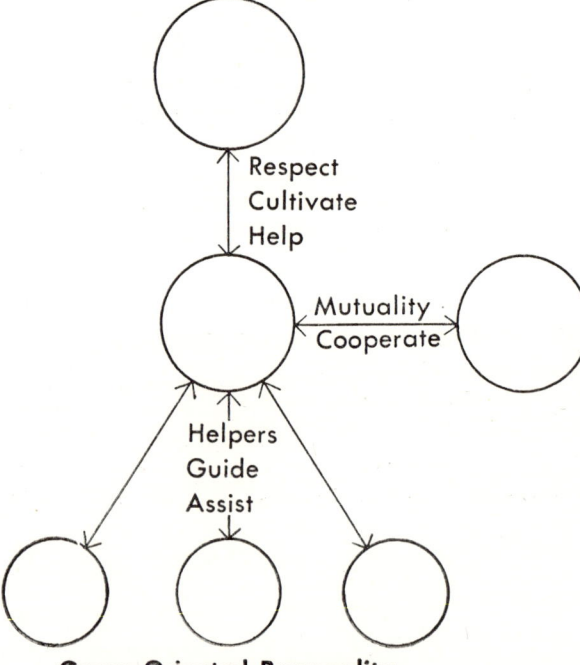

Respect
Cultivate
Help

Mutuality
Cooperate

Helpers
Guide
Assist

Group-Oriented Personality

Relations with Superiors

Describing the problems of working under an authoritarian superior, Learned, Ulrich and Booz observe that "Cultivation of the proper approach to the 'boss' or the 'old man' may become the junior's primary and most absorbing task—a process requiring infinite skill, pains, and patience."[8] This description fits perfectly in the Mexican scene. The chief difference between the United States and the Mexican situations is that what Learned and his associates reported as an undesirable deviation from the United States cultural norm is the common experience in Mexico, as it is in other countries where authoritarian systems are dominant. Since the individual has been living under authoritarian systems all his life, he has usually developed much more "skill, pains, and patience" than his counterpart in the United States. Furthermore, of great significance to the United States executive is the fact that, most superiors in his society being authoritarian, the Mexican tends to approach any relationship with a superior with that expectation and conducts himself accordingly.

Some executives in an authoritarian system lack initiative and seem concerned only with figuring out their superiors' desires and conforming to them. As Mr. Ramirez' remarks (p. 25) about the father-son relationship suggest, however, the man who becomes an executive is usually not the man who has meekly submitted to superior authority. The attitudes of the individualistic executive toward his superiors are likely, therefore, to be a combination of awe and disrespect.

Because of his potential power, the superior is constantly on the mind of the subordinate. One Mexican executive looked up at the picture of the vice president in charge of the international division which hung on his wall and said, "Sometimes I think he's smiling at me. Sometimes I think he's mad at me. I guess it's mostly a matter of my conscience. Sometimes I know I'm doing the right thing, and sometimes I'm not sure I'm doing the right thing even though I think I am." This executive and others with individualistic tendencies observed in the study were acutely aware of the strength of the superior's position and of his importance in their advancement.

This awe of the superior was not necessarily accompanied by real

---

[8] Edmund P. Learned, David N. Ulrich, Donald R. Booz, *Executive Action* (Boston: Division of Research, Harvard Business School, 1951), p. 59.

respect. In some cases it was, but more frequently the subordinate had reservations about the business competence of the superior and in a still greater number of instances, he showed what can best be called a "human disrespect." That is, he did not view the superior as a person who had capacities for understanding, honesty, and tolerance and could therefore be trusted as a leader and adviser.

These attitudes result in relationships which amount to "dealing with" the superior. The individualistic executive's objective is to keep the superior out of the way as much as possible and to get his approval or support as needed to get the job done, all the while trying to make the boss think well of him. This is no easy task, and the methods observed in the study differed both in pattern and apparent success. They did show certain uniformities, however.

The most common element was the appearance of obedience or agreement. Instructions by the boss were in most cases actually obeyed without discussion even if the executive had doubts about them. If he felt quite strongly in disagreement, he still indicated acceptance. He would then defer action or do enough to convey the impression of conforming without actually accomplishing the superior's full wishes. Where follow-up and control systems were effective, these tactics were not very successful, but they would frequently be attempted, especially delaying tactics, in preference to a direct disagreement with the superior.

In general, this structuring of superior-subordinate relations applies in all authoritarian cultures. The chief variations are in the way the subordinate will act when he disagrees with a superior. An executive with experience in several European countries indicates the range: "In France it is quite common for a subordinate to go ahead and do a job a different way than he had been told, and then come and tell the superior about it. In Italy they will do the same thing except they would not tell the superior. In Germany such action is just not acceptable at all."

There is much greater real submission in Germany, but the instinct against it is strong even there.

> [The Germans] would have liked to have some all-knowing and all-powerful person give them the right answers. They preferred to have individuals in positions of leadership who were strong and sure. On the other hand, they did not want to be ordered around and told what to do. Their ambivalence emerged as a longing for submission to some great inspirational leader, and a

resentment of being asked to submit to the wishes or commands of any other actual human being.[9]

The way in which individualistic Mexican executives handle their relations with superiors is illustrated by the actions of Mr. Hernandez, the head of the maintenance department of the Walker Company. The general manager, Mr. Cole, and the production manager, Mr. Pachuca, both conceived the need to change a system in the maintenance department, though in different directions. Mr. Hernandez also felt a change was in order, but he strongly favored a system quite different from those suggested. When the three men met to discuss the problem, he hinted at his plan a couple of times early in the discussion, but otherwise was silent, while his two superiors engaged in a free-swinging argument over their ideas. After the meeting he expressed confidence that he could deal with the problem, "All I can do is hope they'll wear themselves out in arguing about it and then they'll hand it back to me. Let them talk and get it off their chests, and eventually I'll bring them around to some of my ideas. You know, what you want to do is to listen to the other fellow and take in some of his ideas so that he thinks you're accepting them, and then start working him around slowly to your ideas. If they don't wear themselves out right away, I'll just keep dragging my feet till they do."

The immediate effect of Mr. Hernandez' tactics was apparent in the impressions of the two superiors as reported after the meeting. The general manager was quite sure, on the basis of a talk several weeks earlier, that Mr. Hernandez agreed with him, but he felt he had been a little partial to the production manager's point of view in the meeting. This, he concluded, was only natural, since the production manager was his immediate boss. The production manager had no doubts about Mr. Hernandez agreeing perfectly with him.

There was one notable break in this pattern which represents an adjustment to conceptions of modern management. The astute, individualistic executive has learned that the complete "Yes-man" is not considered a good subordinate. Therefore, part of dealing effectively with the boss is to disagree with him sometimes. The choice of when, where, and on what points to disagree is an important one, however. Some executives were quite skilled in this art. Mr. Sanchez, for example, was observed to be adept at picking moments when the boss

[9] Ronald Lippitt and Jeanne Watson, *op. cit.*, p. 24.

was in an amiable mood to disagree with him on specific operational points in a field where the boss felt secure enough not to worry if he gave a little ground. While there were several significant points on which Mr. Sanchez did not agree with his superior, he kept these to himself. His success in "dealing with" the boss was attested to by the boss's report that "Mr. Sanchez is very honest. Whenever he has something on his mind, he comes in and talks it over with me."

Dealing with the orders and ideas of the boss was the main concern of executives with individualistic personalities. Beyond that, they were usually happy to work alone and not be bothered by superiors. From time to time, however, situations arose in which action or approval from above was needed. Sometimes, of course, the superior would be prepared to agree, but this could never be taken for granted, and a negative response would be a major setback. Therefore, considerable thought would be devoted to developing plans of attack.

Mr. Cortez felt one of his assistants would be better off in another job. He didn't know that his boss, Mr. Flicker, felt the same way, so he set about making his plans. "This is something that I've wanted to do for some time. It took me a while to work it out, though. I had to wait for my chance to see how I could approach Mr. Flicker on it. I had to think about it for quite a while. I was trying to figure out some approach to him when it came to me one day. He had been telling me that he didn't think the Kawker Company was being fair to Mr. Gonzales, that they were loading him up with more work than he could handle. So right there, in a flash, it came to me that that was the way to approach him. So a couple of days later I came up to him and laid it right on the line. I said to him, 'Do you remember what you were saying to me the other day about Kawker not being fair to Gonzales?' He said, 'Yes.' And I said, 'Do you think you're being fair to me?' And he said, 'Well, what do you mean?' and I said, 'Do you think you're being fair to make me work with an organization that I don't want?' and then I told him about the organization I thought we should have and he said, 'O.K., go ahead with it.' So, you see, I had him there. He had no way out. I really had him so he had to approve."

The relationship of the group-oriented personality with his superior starts from a different attitude, at least where the superior himself is a competent man with a similar personality. In such a relationship genuine respect both for the ability and the human qualities of the superior is usually found in the executive. He sees the superior as a person who fills an essential part of his life in guiding his efforts, helping him to grow, and making possible the group accomplishments out of which come his own satisfactions. He tries, therefore, to bring himself close to the superior, helping him and being helped in turn.

Mr. Salinas had this point of view. He'd been put in charge of developing a series of new programs under the general direction of Mr. Jones, a man with long experience in his field. Both men had essentially group-oriented personalities and Mr. Salinas had found the relationship a rewarding one: "I've had a good teacher. You see, Mr. Jones is a very able man. He has a lot of ideas which help me. When things come up, I go and talk to him and any advice he can give me I've found I can use. I've found he is right most of the time, and so I take his suggestions."

Mr. Salinas' contacts with Mr. Jones followed this pattern. They were fairly frequent and rarely planned in great detail. He had a strong independent streak and considerable respect for Mr. Jones' time, so he didn't bother him unless he felt the matter important. But when he had a problem or something significant came along, talking about it with Mr. Jones was instinctive.

Relations with Subordinates

The differences in the relationships the two types of executives have with their subordinates, shown diagrammatically in Figure 3, are summed up in these remarks by Mr. Jimenez, a Mexican whose attitudes had passed through a notable transition: "When the manager starts out, he does not essentially believe in raising people up beneath him and helping them. He wants men under him who will do exactly what he wants. He may adopt a variety of practices like personnel administration, but these are adopted with a manipulative attitude, not to make people grow, but rather to permit him to exercise his control more broadly. When he gets in a bigger organization, he realizes he can't do it himself. He must set up a system so that he can delegate work and these are part of the system he sets up, but he doesn't have any real feel for it as a way to develop other people. This is the way it was with me. I tried to find men I could trust below me who would carry out my orders. I started to delegate to them and then I found they started to grow and become more effective people. I realized that something more important than just extending my control was involved."

My research indicated that in Mexico and most of the world, the initial attitudes of this executive are still the dominant ones. Subordinates are viewed essentially as tools in the hands of the superior. They are often seen as unreliable and untrustworthy tools who have to be kept in their places, lest they either do poorly and make the boss look bad, or do well and take the boss's job away from him. In the mind of an executive with a kindly nature, these feelings may be submerged, but they are still strong. Mr. Guzman (page 15), for example, spoke about liking to help men learn and get ahead. But his real feelings were much more in evidence when he expected his subordinates to stand correctly at attention, flipping over pages for him to sign; when he talked about the years of learning which were essential to his job and which no young man could get from a book; and especially when he spoke in troubled terms of the man who had been brought in to do part of his work. He found some consolation in the fact that, "Although he probably can do the job better than I now, I was the pioneer in developing it." Still, the fact that someone could come in and so quickly and easily take over part of his job disturbed him greatly.

As Mr. Jimenez observes, the magnitude of large operations forces executives to delegate and adopt other measures which have potentialities for giving subordinates greater freedom and opportunity to grow. The wide dissemination of such "modern management" concepts as decentralization and executive development provides a further incentive for the "modern executive" to adopt these practices. The structure and the terminology is often found, therefore, but the underlying attitudes of the Mexican individualistic culture remain and set the tone for the real relationships with subordinates.

Mr. Torres was eager to be a "modern executive" and with the best of intentions did many things to achieve delegation, personnel development, and good communications. Something was lacking, however. He felt it was important to understand his men: "They won't talk unless you really prove to them that you are willing to listen to them. You have to make that very clear. I make it clear that my door is open all the time to people who want to come in. Men may come anytime. They may come in at five o'clock with some problem on their minds. Now, one thing you want to do is handle the thing right. If a man comes in, he may want to sit right down and talk about what's on his mind. But that's not the way you want to do it. I want him to bring the subject up the right way. I say, 'Now, let's take our time. Have a cigarette. Let's talk about this week's bullfight for a few minutes.' Then we can get down to talking about the problem, and the man's a little more relaxed." And many of the men by then had lost the nerve that had carried them into the inner sanctum in the first place so Mr. Torres found elaborate efforts were needed to find out what was on men's minds. In some difficult cases he hired the friend of an assistant to take the assistant to dinner and report back what he could learn.

Mr. Torres wanted to train men and delegate to them, but he never could really give up the sense of control he felt or develop faith in his men or feel satisfaction in their accomplishments. He kept hovering over them, seeing training as a process of injecting his own skills into them. "I see that the men have meetings of their own staffs. I don't make them do it, you understand, but I encourage it and I go around and attend them whenever I can. I don't say anything, of course, but after the meeting, if I see something's been done wrong, then I call the manager in and I tell him that such and such a thing wasn't explained right. That way, we build the organization up to run better." And, of a man whose section was not functioning well, "I kept telling him where I thought he ought to direct his energy."

Quite a few new ideas and methods had come out of Mr. Torres' department. While he was undoubtedly the chief innovator in the group, other men had played a big part in these ideas. Mr. Torres did not talk about their role, however. He spoke only in terms of "I have the ideas." When he talked about his men it was either to discuss their shortcomings or sometimes his methods of getting them behind his plans. For example, he described how he got a stubborn section chief to cooperate with a new method. "There was one man who was a real problem. Now, I'll tell you how I sold him. I went around to him a few days ago and I told him, 'You know, by gosh, I finally sold top management that idea of yours. I got them to approve that change you suggested a couple of years ago.' He said he had forgotten about that, but he didn't really remember, you know. Now he thinks that it was his idea and he's all in favor of it."

Thinking back to the previous section, we can visualize how the section chief may have taken all of this and it will come as no surprise that when the change was actually put in, it ran into considerable resistance among men in the section and the section chief showed little interest in straightening out the trouble.

The thing that was missing in Mr. Torres' approach was clearly present in the relationships of Mr. Avila, a man whose attitudes tended strongly in the group-oriented direction. Mr. Avila's subordinates were helpers without whose support he knew neither he nor the company could progress. Furthermore, he liked them and they liked him, from the gateman whom he patted on the back every morning to Mr. Juarez, the quality-control manager, whom he kidded about the bad lot that slipped by the day before. Letting a bad lot slip by was not really a joking matter to Mr. Avila, but he knew it hurt the pride of Mr. Juarez and he was pretty sure that Juarez would really chase after the cause of that slip.

The way Mr. Avila handled a problem in one of his production units gives a good picture of how he managed his men. When the unit was set up, a man was brought in from the outside to run it. He was an expert in the field, but production lagged and he showed little interest in getting in and straightening out the problems. Therefore he was fired, and Mr. Diaz, a young man from another section of the company, was put in the job. Mr. Diaz could not get things going, either, and Mr. Avila soon realized that he had a real problem which he corrected with characteristic honesty and fairness. "That's a case in which I made a bad mistake. I threw a green man in there. I didn't know anything about the business. I thought he could just go in and start to run it, but it didn't work. He got very bad results and he was getting deeper and deeper into trouble, not knowing what to do about it. So finally, I sent him away for a month and a half to our plant in the States.

"I sent him away for three reasons. First, to learn technical information; second, to learn about productivity; and third, just to get away from here. What he could learn in a month and a half in the way of technical skill is small. I knew that. The productivity was more important. He'd never been outside Mexico. I wanted him to get up to the United States and see what sort of standards were possible in the way of what men could produce, and how many machines they could tend, and how high a wage you could pay them and raise their standard of living.

"But the most important thing was just to get him out of here so that he'd have a chance to clear his head and get away from the confusion. He just wasn't doing any good over there. I couldn't fire him. It was my mistake in putting him over there, not his, so I had no right to blame him. But I had to get him out of there, and then I could go in myself and see what could be done. I didn't know anything about the business, but I found out that just by going over there and patting the men on the back and keeping an eye on them, helping them along, things started to move up steadily. Well, that's a demonstration that's important for him. He can see now what can be done, even without knowing all of the technical side."

When Mr. Diaz returned, Mr. Avila would not let him near the plant for a week, continuing to supervise the unit, even though his other work was piling up. "I want to give him time to think out all his ideas and make up his plans, before he gets embroiled in the details over here." Avila had been thinking a lot about how Diaz should work into the supervision again. He had a quite complete plan in mind which would permit him to turn over the whole job to Diaz in two weeks. After Diaz and Avila had talked together, however, Avila reported, "Now we've set up a program. He worked it up himself, just exacty what he wanted to do. I looked it over and made a few notes on it, but he's going to start in on one department and then go on to the next and so on till after two months, he's worked through them all. I'm going to stay with him until he has that picture and can handle the whole thing."

Whether Diaz' plan was actually a sound one or whether he would, in fact, prove able to run the unit, one cannot say. The significant part of the story is the feeling which Mr. Avila had for Diaz and the willingness to give him an opportunity, to guide him, and to see him through. These are the characteristics which distinguish the group-oriented personality in dealing with subordinates.

The Patron-paternalistic Relationship

Paternalistic attitudes are strong in most parts of the world and they are therefore an important influence in the relationships discussed in the previous two sections. They are considered separately, however, because the points of view of the individualistic and group-oriented personalities toward them do not show the same contrasts.

In the course of this research men of both types were observed who looked upon their superiors as *patrones* with the characteristic sense of dependency. They expected the boss to take a responsibility for their lives, to be concerned about their families, to do extra things for them when they were sick, and so forth. The strength of these feelings did vary, but the differences seemed to be due more to differences in the character of the superior than to the degree of grouporientedness in the subordinate. Where the superior showed a willingness to assume a paternalistic responsibility, the subordinate usually showed considerable dependency, and along with it a sense of loyalty.

The deeper significance of these bonds did vary according to the personalities involved. For the individualistic personality they assumed the same character as friendships and alliances (p. 27). For the group-oriented personality the bonds had stronger personal meaning. In practical terms, however, the expectations of responsibility from the superior and willingness to render loyalty were similar.

Likewise, in their relations with their own subordinates, executives of both types showed a notable sense of paternalistic responsibility. In this respect the group-oriented executive differs notably from a comparable type in the United States, where paternalism is generally held in low repute. The current persistence of this attitude in Mexico is due to the expectations of the men's subordinates and the pressures for it from the cultural ideology.

Relations with Nonlinear Associates

There are striking differences in the relationships which the individualistic and group-oriented personalities develop with nonlinear associates (e.g., executives in other departments and staff men). As the broken line in Figure 3 indicates, the individualistic personality does not regard these relationships as a continuing process. He avoids them so far as possible. When they are forced upon him, he approaches them in a highly competitive frame of mind, fighting and maneuvering to win his points, which often means getting the boss to take his side. To the group-oriented personality such relationships are an essential part of life. He usually has a strong sense of the individuality of his department's functions and a competitive desire to advance himself and the department's interests. However, his instincts for sharing and for group activity result in suppressing to some degree his competitive drives in the interest of other company activities. Therefore, he approaches these relationships with a sense of mutuality of objectives and an urge to cooperate.

The words of one Mexican executive describe the essence of the attitude of the individualistic personality in nonlinear relationships.

"We fight a constant battle against departmentalism. Our big problem down here is understanding other people and not getting emotionally involved. You know how the Mexican is. We get our own idea and that's all we can see. We argue for it like mad, and then our pride gets involved. So we get stubborn, and then maybe finally we have to accept the other guy's point of view but we don't do it gracefully. We sniff and say, 'Well, all right, if we've got to do it that way, we've got to do it.' But we don't really believe in it."

The overriding interest of the individualistic executive is to advance himself and his department by whatever means he can. For a Mexican this may lead to emotional arguments or to tricky maneuvers. For people from other cultures the method may be different. But given the individualistic personality, the attitude is usually similar. For example, Lippitt and Watson observe of a group of Germans: "The idea of interdependence and mutuality of influence and responsibility was lacking. . . . To accept somebody else's idea was to be defeated and to be a conformist." [10]

These attitudes tend to be self-reinforcing among a group of executives with similar personalities. Each avoids the others and in doing so confirms their opinion that he has neither interest in nor knowledge of their work. The following quotations are typical. A production manager: "Now we've got a lot of people around here who don't know the plant and don't know our problems, so I had to really push to get my plan across. Take the people in finance, for example. They're all pesos there. They can't visualize that maybe you'll spend a thousand pesos and get five thousand of better production back. I don't think the treasurer knows anything about production. I don't think in all the time I've been here I've ever seen him out in the plant." And the treasurer, dealing with a credit financing problem about which the sales manager had shown little interest in a staff meeting said, "Oh, he understands the problem all right, but he doesn't care. You see, he's just responsible for selling. But it's all right. The general manager understands and when the moment comes he will make the decision to limit credit."

The tone of the treasurer's remarks is interesting because of its sense of acceptance. To him this state of affairs was natural and not undesirable. That point of view is typical of the individualistic personality. Running one's own department without involvement with outsiders is simpler and more satisfying. When disputes arise there will

[10] Ronald Lippitt and Jeanne Watson, "Some Special Problems of Learning and Teaching Process in Cross Cultural Education." Paper delivered at International Congress of Psychology, June, 1954, p. 18.

be a fight, but in the end it will be resolved by the superior. And so long as he is reasonably fair, the executive is content, though if the decision goes against him, he may be emotionally upset for a while.

The following incident in the Paris Company indicates fairly common actions and reactions. Mr. Fernandez, the sales manager, was anxious to push sales of one product above the level of planned production for the following month. The production manager, Mr. Morelos, was away when Mr. Fernandez conceived his plan and he went directly to the chief of the scheduling section and told him the output of the product should be increased, other schedules being reduced to free the necessary facilities. The scheduling chief refused to act till Mr. Morelos returned the following Thursday. When he returned, Mr. Morelos decided quite definitely that the change was unacceptable because disrupting the schedule would raise costs and unbalance his labor utilization plan. He did not communicate with Mr. Fernandez, however, believing that the general manager was well disposed toward him and that his best course of action was to make his points at the staff meeting next morning.

He prepared a concise statement of the effects of the change, and when he had a chance, presented it to the meeting. Mr. Fernandez then gave his arguments expressing some doubts that the results would be as bad for production as Mr. Morelos implied. There followed a civil but fairly strong debate between the two. After several exchanges, the general manager entered into the discussion, generally supporting Mr. Fernandez. This disturbed Mr. Morelos considerably and he became rather emotional in predicting serious difficulties for the future if schedules were changed every time sales had a new idea. The general manager cut the discussion off shortly thereafter, instructing Mr. Morelos to make the change.

Mr. Fernandez was, of course, pleased with the outcome. "You see, we have our fights, our little squabbles. But we take them up to the manager and he decides. Sometimes he decides one way, sometimes another. This time, you see, he was on my side." Mr. Morelos was quite perturbed by the decision. He talked to the general manager privately after the meeting and tried to get the decision changed. When this effort failed he had the schedules revised, but he was unable to talk about the situation for several days without getting emotionally upset.

Though these relations are distant, competitive, and often characterized by bitter fights, that does not mean that the individuals are enemies or feel continuing personal animosity. This may appear inconsistent but it is part of the individualistic executive's attitude toward people. Given his generalized distrust and hostility to all people, he finds nothing unusual in relationships such as we have just seen. Some of the individualistically inclined executives observed that they were good friends with other executives, which did not seem consistent with the content of their relationships. What they meant was that they were able to have amiable social contact with the men, and this, to them, was all that friendship involved, a point that relates to Beals' comments on Mexican friendships (page 27).

The nonlinear relations which the group-oriented personality tends to develop are not easy to describe because they include intangible feelings and mutual confidence which develop gradually, in contrast with the sharply-defined intermittent interactions of the individualistic type. However, by looking carefully at one fairly representative executive, we may get a sense of the content of these relationships.

Mr. Flores was a controller and thus had contact with all of the departments of the company. He conceived his role as that of protecting the company's financial position, which included cutting costs, limiting expenditures, and making sure that prices were high enough to produce a profit. He pursued this role with great energy and was frequently referred to as "old money bags" by other executives. They accepted his function readily, taking comfort in the assurance that he had his eye on the financial situation, leaving them free to concentrate on their functions. Whenever there was a problem which involved costs or prices, he would be called in to give his views, which he did with the greatest vehemence.

On his own initiative he undertook various campaigns and individual battles to keep costs down. For example, he had observed that materials were a large portion of the company's costs and that waste seemed rather high. He felt that the production people were not sufficiently interested in the problem, so he drew up some charts to prove his points and after getting the general manager and production manager interested, he gave a lecture on the subject to all the production supervisors. After a few months the campaign showed significant results and he asked the general manager to give a dinner for the production group at which both he and the manager made speeches praising the results.

Mr. Flores was inclined to attribute much of his success to circumstances. He'd been with the company since it was quite small and he felt this had given him a chance to get to know the people and the operations. Undoubtedly circumstances had been favorable for him, but the relationships which he had developed seemed to have more to do with what he had made of the circumstances than the circumstances themselves.

In earlier years the company had no sales manager and both the general manager and production manager were often away on sales trips, leaving Mr. Flores as the only executive in the office. Problems had come up in the plant which the supervisors had not felt able to solve. They had taken to bringing them to Mr. Flores. He usually did not feel able to solve them, but he helped the men to think out solutions and occasionally made decisions himself. He told the production manager what he had done as soon as he returned, and apparently the latter was usually satisfied with what had happened and appreciated Flores' efforts.

Thus people got used to his being involved in the work of other departments. He became known as a man who was always sympathetic and responsible in his attitude toward the problems of others. They sensed that whatever he did he intended for the good of the company and not for himself alone. This understanding was something that had to be built gradually with each individual in the company by repeated tests and reinforcements in specific actions. And it is questionable if he would have been so successful, if he had not been in a group, most of whom showed the same attitudes. His associates took great pride in the fact that they never did anything without being sure that they had consulted with everyone else who might be interested and, when two men were forced to refer a disagreement to the general manager for arbitration, that was regarded as something of a defeat and clearly an exceptional circumstance.

The physical differences between Mr. Flores' relationships and those of the individualistic type are readily evident: the frequent interaction with other departments, the direct approach to problem solving on the spot rather than looking always to the superior for decisions, and the general goodwill in the relationships. But the essence of the approach lies in the underlying feelings which start with the man himself: his orientation toward the good of the company as a whole, his sympathy with the problems of others and desire to help them, and his straightforwardness. These qualities stimulate the trust and fellow feeling of others which are essential to assure the cooperation he needs to be effective in his job.

THE INDIVIDUALISTIC PERSONALITY IN A CHANGING ENVIRONMENT

The individualistic personality, as we saw earlier, was the product of the traditional Mexican environment. That environment has been changing gradually over the last 50 years and it seems clear that the culture is changing with it. Perhaps the best evidence lies in the number of younger executives who show at least to some degree, and in some instances to a high degree, the attitudes of the group-oriented personality. It seems likely, therefore, that elements of the group-oriented personality will gradually be absorbed into the culture and an increasing number of men with group-oriented attitudes will be available for executive positions. The process is a slow one, however, and, from a practical point of view, the United States executive must live with the type of men who are available today.

Observing the relationships which the individualistic personality develops, one cannot escape the conclusion that executives with these characteristics are not so effective in administrative relationships as men with group-oriented personalities. That does not mean, however, that they cannot be valuable as executives. Most of the men observed in this study showed strong individualistic tendencies and yet were useful to their companies. Whole organizations exist in which relationships of the individualistic type predominate and which are notably effective. Therefore, the United States executive needs to look carefully at the attitudes and relationships of these executives against the setting of the foreign environment and be prepared to adjust his own concepts of administration so as to make the most effective use of the men.

In doing so he faces a number of specific problems. What men should he select as executives? To what extent should he accept their attitudes? How should he set up his own methods to utilize them effectively? The answers to these questions which were observed in this study were extremely varied and it did not appear from analyzing their results that there were any clear rules which could be followed. To a large extent the approaches of the executives were intuitive, being a part of their general attitude toward the foreign culture and the administrative attitudes it produced. It did appear, however, from observing the character of the organizations in which different types of approaches were common, that there were general

criteria which would be helpful to a United States executive in thinking out his own attitudes in meeting such problems.

As a starting point, we may distinguish two criteria for the success
of an organization: first, its effectiveness in achieving company objectives (e.g., sales and profits); and, second, its success in satisfying
the objectives of its members (e.g., personal income and prestige).
The problems faced by United States executives often appeared as
a simple choice between these two criteria, but that was a dangerous
oversimplification because a variety of factors were usually relevant
to both.

Operating Effectiveness

A large portion of the United States executives interviewed in this
study spoke of attitudes of foreign executives which reduced the
effectiveness of their companies. Poor communications, failure to develop subordinates, and other characteristics observed earlier in this
chapter provided numerous examples. The study gave no basis for
questioning their opinions in absolute terms.

In terms of human realities, however, there seemed to be a significant argument that effectiveness was furthered by tolerating at
least some of these attitudes. It will be evident from the discussion
in Chapter Five that changing culturally-based attitudes is a slow
process. To attempt to accelerate the change by pressure, or to force
actions counter to strongly-held attitudes, usually creates strains in
relations with foreign executives. They may react in various ways,
including, as one executive put it, "Killing you off by the tortoise
treatment." It may, therefore, be well to accept a somewhat lower
level of administrative effectiveness than might otherwise be desired
to preserve the over-all effectiveness arising from the mental state of
people.

A further element in the total picture is the relative importance of
various types of skills. Taking a historical perspective, it appears that
in industrial evolution technical skills develop earlier than administrative skills. This was true in the growth of United States industry
and it is evident in Mexico today. In this study a number of Mexicans were observed who were competent in engineering, selling, and
other technical skills. Many of them were also quite advanced in the
capacities discussed in the next chapter—creativity, analytical thoroughness, and so forth. However, the competence of most of these

men in administrative relationships was at a considerably lower level. In many of these cases it seemed best to tolerate the latter to get the greatest benefit of the former.

Mr. Gonzales, the sales manager of one United States subsidiary, is a good example. Mr. Gonzales was a man of tremendous drive and great imagination. He was constantly thinking up new ideas which were effective in raising the company's sales to a high level. In his work Mr. Gonzales appeared as something of a prima donna. He offended other executives and did not have very effective relations with his subordinates.

Mr. Morgan, the manager of the company, took a relatively tolerant attitude toward the administrative deficiencies of all of his men. He encouraged improvement by rewarding those who cooperated well, did good training jobs, and so forth, but he did not push the men hard in these directions. In terms of the total effectiveness of the operation, this policy seemed sound. If Mr. Gonzales had become fully aware of his deficiencies and become greatly concerned about correcting them, he might well have lost much of his creative effectiveness.

Such a conclusion is hard to reach because it rests upon evaluation of a great variety of characteristics both in the man and in the whole administrative situation. The point of view, however, is an important one to consider in a country like Mexico, where men with advanced technical skills are still not very common and the full utilization of these skills may contribute more to company effectiveness than refinements of administrative skills.

Another consideration in evaluating an executive's effectiveness is his skill in his relationships with his countrymen, both within and outside of the company. The essence of this problem was summed up by one United States executive, "We have to guard against hiring men who can work well with us rather than men who can work well with other Mexicans." As long as the Mexican culture is as it is, the majority of the contacts of a Mexican executive are likely to be with men with individualistic personalities. If he is to be effective, it is important that he be able to understand them and do business in their way.

Some men are capable of being truly bi-cultural in that they can wholeheartedly apply two different types of attitudes and values, depending on the situation in which they find themselves. For example, Mr. Smith was essentially straightforward in his dealings with his close associates. Over many years, however, he had learned to deal effectively with the shrewd Mexican businessmen outside his company. Not only was he highly effective in his relations with them, but to these relations he applied their values, not his. As he said, when asked if he felt angry when one of them outsmarted him, "Oh, I get mad all right. That's why I take these (indicating his digestion pills). But not at him. There's no reason to be mad at him. I get mad because I let him trick me. I should know better. I've lived here for years and I shouldn't get tricked by one of these things." Some Mexican executives have the same ability to live by the standards of two cultures, but it is not common. There is a danger, therefore, of selecting men who are effective organizational types but who are so alienated from their own society that they do not function in it effectively. Turning to another country, the Useems quote an Indian who had run squarely into this problem.

Father [the owner of a large industrial plant] says, "You have ideas that won't work in India; your method is too quick, your mind is American but your heart is Indian"—and he is right. People in business take advantage of me and I am never sure when they are doing so or what I should do to stop them. I don't know how to bargain. I don't know whether, if I do a man a favor, he will do me a favor. I don't know when to believe a man in India, or whom to trust. One of our agents cheated me and I don't know why he did it. Should I keep him? Should I accuse him?— I am at a complete loss. I feel incompetent. Father would know what to do. I don't. I always try to keep my word. Indians make promises—any promises—whether they intend to keep them or not. I use written contracts. Indians use notes and letters and they say my contracts are ridiculous. Indians run down their competitors, for this is a principle of fair practice. I have instructed my staff never to say bad things about other people's stock and they think this is more American foolishness.[11]

Satisfying Individual Desires

Evaluating the administrative attitudes in terms of effectiveness in satisfying human desires still further complicates the situation. It is important because the satisfactions which a man achieves from his work have much to do with the energy and initiative which he shows

[11] John Useem and Ruth Hill Useem, *The Western-Educated Man in India* (New York: The Dryden Press, 1955), p. 38.

on the job. In one way or another most competent United States executives felt as one man said specifically, "We want the people to be happy here." This is no weak-minded benevolence. As we will see in Chapter Six, sensitivities common among foreign executives must be intelligently countered if good working relations are to be established. This point of view leads frequently to a tolerant attitude toward the administrative attitudes of foreign associates. When a man's culturally-based attitudes are challenged, he is usually not happy. If he is used to doing things in a certain way, he will be more comfortable if he can continue to accomplish his ends in the same manner. This simple observation was confirmed repeatedly in the study. Mr. Gonzales (page 49), for example, was on the whole happy in his work because he was succeeding on the basis of his creativity and selling skill, and his administrative deficiencies were not directly challenged by Mr. Morgan.

Furthermore, the foreign executive may prefer the discomforts of his accustomed pattern of relationships to the uncertainties of a new pattern, even though the latter is apparently more favorable to him. The classic example is the change from an authoritarian to a democratic superior. Some men appreciate the change, but in other cases the subordinate is baffled by the change and uncertain how to conduct himself in the new relationship. He then expresses a preference for the "old system" under which he at least knew where he stood. This type of attitude has been observed in other contexts. For example, Lambert's studies of Indian students who had acquired an understanding of United States family life revealed that despite an ideological preference for liberal relationships, they preferred the strictly-structured, tightly-knit Indian family.[12] They felt more at ease because the role of each member was well established and confusion and uncertainty in relationships were reduced to a minimum, even though the relationships might at times be unpleasant for the individual. From the point of view of personal satisfaction, therefore, much is to be said for accepting the administrative attitudes of the foreign executive.

There is another side to this story. In the first place, however familiar the executive may find the traditional relationships, he is not always happy in them. We have already observed in the case of Mr.

[12] Richard D. Lambert and Marvin Bressler, "Indian Students and the United States," *The Annals* (Philadelphia: The American Academy of Political and Social Science), September, 1954, p. 64.

Morelos the type of emotional disturbance they can produce (page 44). The chief problem lies in the frustration which may develop in relations with the superior. A case in point was the situation of Mr. Alcaraz. Some difficulties had developed in Mr. Alcaraz' department. His superior was putting strong pressure on him to correct the trouble, indicating his own opinions as to the causes. Mr. Alcaraz did not fully agree about the causes and he was intensely worried about the problem. He was unable to communicate these feelings to his superior, however, so he stewed unhappily in his own juice and eventually boiled over in an outburst directed at an assistant.

In the second place, the United States executive is not the only source of challenge to the individualistic attitudes. The general environment and the man's immediate administrative situation are persistent and far less tactful challengers. In Appendix A the way cultural attitudes lag behind the requirements of a changing environment is discussed along with the mental stresses that the lag produces. Mr. Gonzales is a typical example (page 49). While he was, in general, satisfied with his life, he was constantly aware that the administrative process was not functioning well. Although he wanted to be a good administrator, he was unable to see his administrative actions as others saw them, and he usually rationalized the problems which developed as due to the shortcomings of his associates. Still, beneath the surface, he was vaguely uncertain and worried about his own adequacy.

On the other hand, men who have acquired attitudes which are effective in administrative action seem to be happier in their work. In striking contrast to Mr. Gonzales was another Mexican sales manager. While he was equally creative and energetic, he was able to conduct his relations with others in such a way that they cooperated with him and he stimulated their efforts. This man was extremely happy in his work and highly effective for the company.

Again, therefore, we are faced with a problem which can be answered only case by case on the basis of the individual feelings of each executive. In the short run, a man will usually be more comfortable if he can live by his instinctive attitudes. In the long run, some change in these attitudes may lead to greater satisfaction. While he is changing, however, he will probably go through periods of considerable distress.

Summary

In this chapter the contrast in attitudes, values and administrative relationships between the individualistic and group-oriented types of personalities has been explored at length. In conclusion, it is well to return to the objectives of the study set forth in Chapter Two. What does the contrast mean for the United States executive?

To some extent it is an educational challenge. Despite many qualifications, encouraging the development of the group-oriented type of attitudes does seem desirable. There are possibilities for change and in Chapter Five we will discuss the ways in which the process may be advanced.

Intriguing though this prospect may be for the United States executive, the greater meaning of the contrast lies in the modification of his expectations. A man with an essentially individualistic personality will act according to that pattern and at best change slowly. The real challenge for the United States executive is to understand the pattern—to be able to interpret the behavior of the man as he talks with him and to predict his performance in his relationships with others in the organization. Out of this understanding the United States executive can then develop a pattern of action of his own which will produce results and not leave him confused by the actions of his foreign associates, in turn confusing and worrying them and all the time not getting results on important business tasks.

Chapter 3

Individual Work

Administrative relationships are necessary to blend the efforts of an organization of specialists into an effective whole. But they are not economically valuable in themselves. The marketable output of the organization depends upon individual productive work—hammering nails, designing machines, planning advertising layouts, developing financial budgets, and a host of other activities. These tasks are often performed by groups of men, so administrative relations are essential to them, but the character of the output of each individual is the raw material which sets limits on the group accomplishments.

As a man progresses up the management ladder, less of his time is usually spent on individual work and more on administrative relations. The complexity and importance of the individual work grows, however, so it remains a significant part of his life. This is especially true of the United States and foreign executives in the overseas operations of United States companies. A very heavy demand for individual output usually falls on their shoulders. The political and economic conditions in foreign countries create a wide range of difficult operating problems. Thousands of miles from the home office, the local management must handle these problems with little help from the senior executives and staff experts of the parent company. Furthermore, in the less developed countries, the executives' subordinates often lack the training necessary to carry a significant share of the load. Thus the attitudes with which foreign executives approach their individual work are of vital concern for the United States executive abroad.

The discussion of these attitudes is complicated because they present a more heterogeneous picture than the attitudes toward people covered in the preceding chapter. There is no single, unifying force in the background comparable to the authoritarian structure of most foreign societies. Thus there is less similarity in attitudes between countries than is the case with administrative relationships, and the various aspects of the way in which a man approaches his work are not interrelated to the same extent.

It is possible, however, to sort out a number of generally observed characteristics and present them as a framework for the executive overseas to use in understanding the problems which he encounters. To facilitate this analysis the individual work of the executive is divided into three phases: innovation, analysis and action. Each of these phases will be discussed in terms of the attitudes with which executives may approach it and the cultural backgrounds of these attitudes.

INNOVATION

The executive is supposed to create. It is not enough that he be a well-oiled gear, keeping the management machine moving in a set pattern. He should introduce new ideas, whether they be novel machine designs, product innovations, or new methods of cost analysis. That is the typical point of view of the United States executive. Coming from a relatively young nation which has glorified the inventive genius, he regards willingness to change and creativity as prime requisites for executive effectiveness. Around the world his point of view comes up against rather strikingly different cultural attitudes, some even more favorable to innovation, and some actively resisting it.

The Mexican culture falls toward the extreme of favorableness to innovation. The comments of both Mexican and United States executives covered by the study testified to this tendency. The remarks of Mr. Silva, a controller, who was, if anything, less creative than many of his associates, are indicative. "Personally, the best satisfactions that I find in the work are the results which I get daily. I like to work at the job and to see the facts developing. I don't like routine work. I like to work and get out the facts and create benefits for the company. Every peso I can save for the company, that's fine. That is where I find my happiness. I'm always thinking, 'How can we cut our costs? What sort of thing can we do to make the best return on our assets?' That's my point of view. Now in other words, I like to make innovations. I like innovations very much. In the States they're always changing ideas in accounting and things like that. These innovations benefit the work which we are doing here. I like to get new ideas."

Mr. Espinosa, a production manager, expressed similar views. "I've never been happy with anything the way it was. I've always tried to see what could be done to improve it."

Mr. Lord, who worked with both executives, observed, "The problem with these men is not to push them to try new things but to hold them back. They are always wanting to do something new."

There were also men who did not show initiative and resisted changes, especially in the lower echelons of management. One executive, after observing a salesman-training course during a visit to the United States, reported his surprise at the number of ideas which the participants produced. He felt that relatively the Mexican salesmen were unimaginative order takers. But this appears to be more a matter of lack of education and opportunity among the lower classes than a general problem of cultural attitudes. The authoritarian structure of Mexican society and the doctrinaire education which will be described in the next section are potentially repressive influences, but despite them, creativity seems to flourish, especially among the upper and middle classes from which most executives are drawn.

Contributing to the attitude of the Mexicans toward innovation are their ethnic background and their history. Mexico today is essentially a *mestizo* nation, most of the people being part Indian and part Spanish. Innovation in different forms is fundamental to both races. The Indians are notable for their artistic creations. The Spanish are full of strong feelings and not much inhibited in expressing them in their physical activities. In the *mestizo* these strains combine to produce an individual who dislikes monotony and has a compelling urge to create. A story which has become a classic in Mexico symbolizes the national psychology. It seems that a worker in a tire factory was found in a corner industriously cutting up the tread of a new tire with a knife. Why? Because he could no longer stand the thought of turning out numberless tires with identical treads.

These tendencies have been supported by the history of Mexico, which is characterized by change and lack of strong national traditions. In 1518 Hernando Cortes with a small band of Spaniards conquered the Aztecs, discrediting thereby the Indian way of life. But the Indians were not swept aside as they were in North America. Instead each race borrowed from the other, developing new patterns of living in everything from religion to agricultural methods. Though the three hundred years after the conquest were relatively stable by comparison with later periods, the country was going through considerable political and economic change.

In 1821 independence was won from Spain and since then Mexican life has been highly unsettled. First, there were fifty years of political upheaval as one group after another tried a new formula for government with approaches ranging from two brief monarchies to a federal democracy. Next came the dictatorship of Porfirio Diaz and a period of political peace, with a major economic revolution. Foreign investors entered the country on a large scale, developing petroleum, minerals and the railroad system; and as the economy expanded, industrialization and urbanization altered the lives of many people. In 1910 Diaz was thrown out and since then the country has been in a state of violent change, with the emphasis in the earlier phase on political evolution and more recently on rapid industrialization. Even religion has not been as much of a stabilizing force as it is in many societies. In 1926 the church was stripped of the great secular power and material wealth it had been accumulating for centuries. For fifteen years thereafter the government was strongly anti-clerical, and to this day the church is sharply restricted in its actions and on the defensive in many respects.

This history has not provided the Mexican with a broad stabilizing tradition. He has learned a way of life which has permitted him to weather the storms: the skills of individualistic living and effective participation in the tight family unit. But these skills are about the limit of tradition in Mexico. Everything else in life has proved relatively unstable, so that change, especially for the urban Mexican, is natural.

Furthermore, Mexicans are quite open to changes coming from outside their country. They have a word for this attitude—*malinchismo*. It is derived from *Malinche*, the name the Indians gave to the Indian woman who became Cortes' wife, and it symbolizes the feeling of the Mexicans that their culture has proved inferior and that they must accept as superior those ideas which come from other nations: religion from Spain, philosophy from France, industrial methods from the United States, and so on. They are not proud of *malinchismo* but they recognize it in themselves, as we see in the following quotation which includes the views of two of the leading observers of Mexican character:

> The Mexican possesses a great power of absorption or adaptation. He is mimetic and has a powerful faculty for imitation. Now when something is imitated, as Samuel Ramos has said, it is because someone believes that it is worthy of imitation, since there exists in the consciousness a previous value judgment which places one's own culture upon a level inferior to that which one attempts to imitate. This is the mechanism of the so-called *malinchismo* and consists, as is well known, in considering everything foreign to be superior simply because it is foreign.[1]

Thus the average Mexican executive is open to innovations. He will accept ideas from the United States, which he willingly recognizes as superior in the field of industrial management. And he is anxious to create new ideas himself. This capacity is a great potential asset. When well directed, it can produce outstanding results. During this research, Mexican executives were observed who had made exceptional contributions in machinery design, financial planning and other fields.

The attitudes toward innovation found in the Mexicans are quite common among peoples who lack long-established traditions, especially those of new nations or areas which have had unsettled conditions for extended periods. Most of the Latin American countries fit this classification.

Where societies have held to established patterns for extended periods, the cultural attitudes toward change are usually quite different. This is true throughout much of Europe and Asia. A transition to new attitudes has started in these areas, but innovation as yet does not have strong cultural support.

In his penetrating analysis of the Asian economic situation, Maurice Zinken puts his finger on the core of the problem in that continent.

> Nearly all economic development involves experiment and change or at least imitating somebody else's change or making use of somebody else's experiments. Countries become richer largely because people are always adopting new methods, learning new techniques, discovering new ways of achieving old

---

[1] Jose E. Iturriaga, *op. cit.*, pp. 240–241.

ends, adapting their lives to new conditions. Nothing is more vital to development than a high propensity to innovate, a high level of willingness to accept and initiate change. The under-development of Asia has to a considerable extent been due to its low propensity to innovate; the Asian peasant learnt how to grow his crops under the conditions of his village two thousand years ago. From then until this generation any experiment he might make was far more likely to end in crop failure and starvation than in riches. Naturally, therefore, Asia puts a heavy emphasis on custom and the ways of one's ancestors, naturally too the road to success has normally been through growing old in conformity.

It is important, therefore, for the development of Asia that the capacity to innovate, especially the capacity to absorb and apply technological knowledge, must be given a higher place than it has been hitherto. There must be built up a class of entrepreneurs, and managers, and successful farmers whose function it is to innovate, whose careers and fortunes depend on their doing so successfully. This is only possible if those who are successful are treated by society with that respect reserved at present for large landowners, great scholars, or senior servants of the State. In any society change is originally the work of the few, though the rest must be prepared to follow; and those few will not become entrepreneurs, or managers, or model farmers, unless to do so gives them the status they feel to be their due. People only apply their minds to inventing better mousetraps when, as De Tocque-ville put it, the world beats a track to the door of those who succeed. In America this track was already being beaten 120 years ago, in De Tocqueville's day; in Asia it is not beaten yet. That is one of the reasons why America is now so rich and Asia still so poor.[2]

Throughout the society pressure and encouragement for innovation are lacking. Describing the traditional attitudes of the people toward change is like describing a vacuum. The concept of change is not present. Life is as it was, is, and will be. It is to be lived as it always has been. The restless state of mind of the United States executive, who is sure that tomorrow will be a great deal different from today and is anxious to get the rewards for making the best changes first, is completely foreign to such a culture.

The attitudes of executives in these cultures are not so bound by inertia as those of the rural peasant. They usually show some degree of interest in change and capacity to innovate. But the extent of these

[2] Maurice Zinken, *Development for Free Asia* (Fair Lawn, N.J.: Essential Books, Incorporated, 1956), pp. 8–9.

attitudes is limited by the society in which they live. What avails it to make a new product, if no one is interested in buying new products; to develop novel advertising schemes, if people will not buy more no matter how much you advertise; or to introduce a new labor management method, if the workers are uninterested and apathetic?

The case of John Macy and Vishnu Rama in Chapter One illustrates the common attitudes. It might be said that Mr. Rama is receptive to change because he has undertaken a new venture in starting to manufacture razor blades. But his lack of interest in pioneering aggressive marketing and advertising methods in India is more significant. Adding a new product to his line is not a major change. His family had added products before. Since razor blades were already on the market, his action did not represent a real innovation, just part of the gradual growth of the business to which he was committed. But aggressive promotion is another story. It involves risks of his money and reputation in return for a chance to make a bigger profit. That prospect does not appeal to him because he is not at heart an innovator.

Mr. Rama's attitudes fit the pattern of Indian industrial society. There are some great Indian industrial empires which testify to the willingness of men to invest in productive enterprise. But these empires are mostly the result of slow and well-considered advancement in basic industries. There are very few examples in Indian industrial history of the pioneering creativity which distinguishes innovators, whether they be inventors like Edison or financial geniuses like Morgan.

To some degree this situation may be due to external forces. India, like many countries, was held in a colonial status over an extended period. British policy was clearly directed at keeping the Indians in a subordinate position. A research team, observing the lack of initiative in Indians of the age group who are now executives, attributes their deficiencies to British education in which, "The stress was on rote memorization rather than on creative inventiveness, on maintenance of equipment rather than on its construction, on the development of an obedient rather than an independent mind." [3] The influence of the British on the relatively limited layer of Indians they educated and supervised was small, however. The main cultural de-

[3] John Useem and Ruth Hill Useem, *The Western-Educated Man in India* (New York: The Dryden Press, Inc., 1955), p. 35.

terrents to innovation have been the pervasive stability and respect for conformity running from top to bottom in the society.

The same sort of stability is found in other societies where the cultural attitudes run against innovation. France, for example, despite changeable politics and intellectual-artistic leadership, is notable for the stolid stability of its peasantry, small merchants and industrial combines. In fact, it appears that the unwillingness of the majority of the population to consider changes in their own lives is a major factor in creating the instability which is so evident in some aspects of French life. For example, the industrialists have been slow to consider changes in production, labor or selling policies which would lead to an expanding mass market and higher standard of living. There has been no Henry Ford in France, willing to cut prices and raise wages in a bold gamble for future expansion. Indeed, one of the great complaints of participants in the productivity programs in France since World War II has been the way most of those French industrialists who did accept cost-cutting production innovations simply pocketed the savings as greater profits. The general attitude of French management has been one of massive resistance to new methods.[4] In Europe one finds a few outstanding management innovators like Gottlieb Duttweiler, whose retailing methods have created a marketing revolution in Switzerland, but the uniqueness of such men confirms the general lack of innovation in the culture as a whole.

There, in broad perspective, is the range of attitudes toward innovation which the United States executive will find among foreign executives—some eager to create and to try new methods brought in from the United States, others unimaginative in their own thinking and reluctant to consider the ideas of others. In the background of these attitudes are cultural influences. Where innovation is encouraged it is usually because traditional patterns of life have not become well-established and innovation has proved both possible and rewarding. Where innovation is discouraged it is usually because tradition has become firmly rooted in the ways of the people and attempts at change meet neither with public acclaim nor material success, conformity being the approved standards for a successful life.

[4] Henry W. Ehrmann, *Organized Business in France* (Princeton, N.J.: Princeton University Press, 1957), pp. 325–340.

ANALYSIS

Analysis is used here to mean both a function and a state of mind. The function is the thoughtful prelude to action, the process in which problems and ideas are organized, examined, and developed in the search for effective patterns of action. The state of mind, the analytical point of view, requires ability to observe and accept reality together with disciplined and orderly logic in thinking. The function and the point of view sum up the essence of scientific management. Their acceptance by United States industry is readily observable in the wealth of books and courses which expound analytical approaches to all phases of work and in the hours and volume of paper devoted to studies and reports. But elsewhere in the world the analytical approach to management is far from accepted. While it appears to be gaining ground, it faces strong opposition from two traditional approaches: established rules and impulse.

In Mexico cultural forces support both these latter approaches so United States executives, applying the standards of analytical management, frequently meet with difficulties and disappointments. A variety of experiences of this sort were observed during the research. In one case, for example, a general manager was having trouble because his sales manager would not analyze promotion schemes. The sales manager seemed to feel that any scheme which was big and colorful was good, and he was unwilling to spend time figuring out its cost, its potential impact and the sales increases it might produce. Another executive could not persuade a personnel manager to develop solutions to some special problems for which he felt the actions prescribed by the existing personnel manual were inappropriate. The personnel manager insisted that they must hold to the procedures in the manual which had been worked out by a group of experts from the home office and therefore represented the approved company approach to personnel management. Problems of this character are not uncommon in the United States. In Mexico, however, they occur more frequently, and overcoming them is more difficult because of the cultural supports behind them.

In understanding these differences in attitudes toward analysis it is helpful to have a picture of the state of mind of various types of individuals. Salvador de Madariaga, in a perceptive description of the national psychologies of the English, French and Spanish, establishes fundamental differences in characteristics which may be usefully applied to the United States-Mexican situation.[5] The United States executive greatly resembles the English, and the Mexican is similar to the Spanish. De Madariaga characterizes the Englishman as the man of action, the Frenchman as the man of thought, and the Spaniard as the man of passion. Extended thought and detailed analysis, he observes, are natural and enjoyable for the Frenchman. This tendency is apparently confirmed by the elaborate schemes which the French have produced in post-war Europe—the Schuman plan, the Monnet plan and so forth.

For men from England and the United States satisfaction, by and large, lies in action. We are nations of doers, not of thinkers. It is not surprising, therefore, to find that scientific management was not eagerly accepted by United States industry. Frank Taylor, whose production analysis methods eventually created a management revolution, reported that nine-tenths of his trouble in the early years was in converting managers who felt confident in their established competence in action.[6] But analysis has a place in this point of view. The doer who wants to get effective results learns in time that careful thinking and planning can contribute to doing a good job. Thus the analytical approach has been adopted as step by step it was proved to managers that it will give them better results.

The man of passion is not essentially concerned with results. Action is an outlet for his emotions. The results may or may not be worthwhile in a utilitarian sense. Their utility is not important. The value of action lies in its effectiveness as a release and a means of expressing inner urges. When the individual has a feeling about something, he wishes to act immediately according to his inclination. With this psychology, the analytical approach is nothing but an impediment. It means that rather than acting according to his feelings, the man must check them against external considerations and in the process, postpone their expression until perhaps they have gone out of his heart.

The other side of the man of passion which is important administratively is that, when he does not have feelings, he is apathetic. Thinking and action in themselves have no particular appeal for him

---

[5] Salvador de Madariaga, *Englishmen, Frenchmen, Spaniards* (London: Oxford University Press, 1929).
[6] Reinhard Bendix, *Work and Authority in Industry* (New York: Renouf Publishing Co., 1956), p. 280.

and he is inclined, therefore, to do things in the manner which requires the least risk and effort. This is where established rules come in. Confronted by a situation in which action is required but about which he has no feelings, the man of passion finds it easiest simply to conform to some existing pattern. If he follows the rules there will be no complaints, he will not have to make a mental effort, and the situation will be taken care of.

The distinction between men of action, thought, and passion is helpful as a starting point in understanding differences in points of view toward analysis. Beyond that, and certainly related to it, are the forces which have affected the mental attitudes of people. The Mexican attitudes go far back in history as Iturriaga observes:

> The Mexican is not very reflective and analytical, coming from two cultures which do not use the rational approach to arrive at the truth. One, the aboriginal, was prelogical, magic, and its supernatural was for it the natural; the other was based on imposition, dogma and faith.[7]

The primitive Indian attitudes have dominated the great masses of the Mexican population for centuries, fostering a national psychology which resists the development of the analytic approach. The Spanish tradition of "imposition, dogma and faith" has deeply influenced the lives of educated Mexicans. Underlying the scientific approach to management is a general philosophy of life which had its origin in the great scientific revolution that swept through most of Europe in the 16th Century on the heels of the Reformation and Renaissance. Hitherto Europeans had largely thought and lived according to dogma handed down through the centuries and usually rigorously enforced by political-religious authority. Then, in a violent upheaval, the authority of both church and state over the minds of men was greatly reduced and the concept that the individual can and should arrive at truth through his own thinking was established.

The religious and political forces in Spain, however, were strong enough to check these revolutionary developments at the Pyrenees and the philosophy of independent, analytical thinking never became part of life in Spain or the lands it colonized. Thus until very recently the prevailing attitude throughout Mexican life has been that it is not the domain of the individual to think about how things should and

---

[7] Jose E. Iturriaga, *op. cit.*, p. 237.

should not be. Rather, he should accept the patterns which are pre-scribed by authorities, whether they be the church, the government, or the personnel experts in the United States.

Mexican education has been geared to this approach. In recent years efforts have been made by educational leaders to introduce practices which develop individual thinking, but they have encoun-tered difficulties in accomplishing their ends because of the pervasive belief that the job of the schools is to indoctrinate the students in "revealed truth." [8] The educational experience of a typical young Mexican provides little opportunity for individual expression or de-velopment:

> In both rural and urban elementary schools, despite the strong influence of John Dewey on Mexican education since the revolu-tion, instruction tends to be authoritarian and to place heavy emphasis upon memory. During study period students learn long passages, repeating them aloud. Consequently, at a distance even a one-room rural school at times will sound like a hive of angry bees. Recitation often consists of the class's repeating in unison passages learned word by word; and final public examinations, which often are oral, may consist of rote responses to fixed questions by the students with the best memories, interspersed with musical selections by the village band and speeches by local dignitaries . . . University instruction tends to be somewhat formal and specialized . . . Lectures tend to be formal and authoritarian. Discussion or case methods have been used only recently and not in all fields. [9]

An additional element in the Mexican culture which limits analyti-cal effectiveness is what is known as *proyectismo. Proyectismo* is not easy to define. It consists essentially of constructing plans without much critical analysis and then assuming the plans to be an accom-plished fact. It includes elements of such common phenomena as day-dreaming and wishful thinking, but goes beyond them in the extent to which the individual is caught up in belief and identification with his schemes as a form of reality. In such a book as this it seems in-appropriate to raise the age-old philosopher's question, "What is reality?" The active executive may be inclined to shunt off such a

[8] George F. Kneller, *The Education of the Mexican Nation* (New York: Columbia University Press, 1951), pp. 64–71.
[9] Ralph L. Beals and Norman D. Humphrey, *No Frontier to Learning* (Minne-apolis: University of Minnesota Press, 1957), pp. 29–30.

question as silly; but in understanding peoples of other cultures it can be a helpful question. *Proyectismo* is part of reality for many Mexicans. Listening to one of them describing a plan, you realize that, however unlikely or uncertain of success the plan may be, the man is experiencing in its conception the same type of satisfactions which a man of action would realize only as he carried it out. And for him the satisfactions are the greater because a plan which exists only in his mind or on paper does not need to suffer the buffeting of conflicts and obstacles. To subject it to that buffeting in advance through the analytical process is therefore to rob it of a large part of its joy.

The origins of *proyectismo* are uncertain. It seems likely that it developed as a compensating element to offset the frustrations of life throughout Mexican history. During the three hundred years of Spanish rule the vast majority of Mexicans lived a servant existence with a meager standard of living and little hope for improvement. As man must have hope and satisfaction to live, the people learned to find pleasure in their dreams and visions of the future. With the coming of independence frustration assumed a national character not just in the lives of individuals, but also at the general political and economic level. In the period from 1821 to 1876 a sequence of new approaches to government organization were attempted. Each one was based on some high ideal and offered great promise for realization of democracy and prosperity. And each one disintegrated into a mess of disorganization and corruption. Eventually, in 1876, the country settled for Porfirio Diaz' harsh dictatorship as the price of political and economic stability, a sad defeat for the ideals of people recently stirred by the democratic principles of Benito Juarez. Democracy was again given room to develop with the removal of Diaz in 1910, but it was not until 1934 that Lazaro Cardenas provided enough strength and stability to set the country firmly on the road to economic and political maturity and the realization of its potentialities. Therefore, from 1821 to 1934, whatever sense of national accomplishment and pride the people experienced came largely from their ability to dream, for there was little satisfaction to be had from their achievements.

Proyectismo, the emotional approach to life, and the respect for dogma combine into a cultural pattern which is inhospitable to analysis. In the extreme they are clearly inconsistent with effective management. Fortunately among executives they usually do not appear as

dominant traits. The men who become executives are the more ana-
lytically oriented and realistic members of the society. Many of them,
being creative and ambitious, are not greatly bound by respect for
dogma and authority. The United States executive does, however,
encounter problems, because most Mexican executives have tendencies in the direction of the cultural traits. The United States executives observed in this study were frequently confronted with situations in which it was necessary to understand the nonanalytical attitudes of their associates and to compensate for them. A specific case
will illustrate the type of situation with which they had to deal.

The Homar Company made a group of consumer products which
were sold through various types of retail stores. When sales in one
class of stores in Mexico City dropped noticeably, the sales manager,
Mr. Riley, became concerned. He talked to Mr. Bustamante, the
manager for the Mexico City district. Mr. Bustamante said he would
get after Mr. Leon, the sub-manager who directed sales in those stores,
to push the salesmen harder. He also felt that more money could be
allotted to advertising the products which were sold heavily in that
class of stores.

Mr. Bustamante called Mr. Leon in the next day and told him about
his talk with Mr. Riley. Mr. Leon said he knew that sales were off and
that this was inevitable because a competitor, Potter Products, had
been engaged in a heavy promotion program, giving sizable increases
in discounts to the stores. As long as that continued, Homar was
bound to suffer unless their discounts were also increased. Mr. Bustamante told Mr. Leon that he could not accept this point of view. An
increase in the discount was out of the question, as the Homar Company had a policy against discount changes. The company had always
succeeded through strong merchandising and effective promotion and
it was up to Mr. Leon to make an additional push to counteract the
competition. He said he was going to see that more money went into
newspaper advertising that would be effective among the class of
people who bought from Mr. Leon's group of stores and this, together
with a stronger selling effort, would do the job. Mr. Leon said it would
not work and furthermore he thought the advertising money should
be held back until the Potter promotion ended, as he was sure it must
fairly soon. Then a strong advertising effort would help Homar re-
cover lost ground. Mr. Bustamante persisted in his position and Mr.
Leon departed, agreeing to do what he could to get sales moving.

Mr. Bustamante made the changes in the advertising program, shifting into the present period a portion of the budget which was to have been spent later in the year on the same media. When he saw Mr. Riley at the end of the day, he said he was sure that his approach would produce results, relating as support some quite exaggerated accounts of the way he had countered competitive promotions in previous years.

Interviewed alone after these talks, Mr. Bustamante expressed his confidence that everything was going to work out all right. He said Mr. Leon was a good man; he needed to get experience and learn how to handle problems like this, but he knew he was going to do the job and sales would soon be back up again.

Mr. Leon did not have the same confidence. He said that Potter had induced the stores to load up on inventory to the point where they could not afford to buy more from Homar. He backed this assertion up with some reports from the salesmen about the size of the stocks some of the stores now had. He used these reports as though they were firm facts, though in a previous interview he had been rather critical of the salesmen for the inaccuracies of the reports they gave him to cover up their performances when their sales were low. He felt that Mr. Bustamante was making a bad mistake on the advertising and that it was futile to push the salesmen hard until Potter ended their promotion.

The expanded advertising program started immediately. A few days later, Mr. Leon came to Mr. Bustamante and asked him to cut it back. He said that the suggestion had come to him from two stores through the salesmen. The store owners said that there had been an increase in demand for the products featured in the advertising and their stocks were running low. They could not possibly order more now because their finances had been stretched to the limit in buying stocks from Potter. They thought it would be to the advantage of both themselves and Homar to postpone the advertising push until they were in a position to buy enough inventory to handle the demand. Mr. Bustamante said that was ridiculous; that the stores would have to learn to manage their finances better and that it certainly proved that his reasoning had been right.

Mr. Leon accepted his decision, but afterwards spoke quite bitterly about the situation. He said that Mr. Bustamante was "putting him on the spot" because it was not going to be possible to sell more to the stores now, and this sort of thing made for bad relations with the store owners.

When the reports on sales for the next month came in, Mr. Leon's prediction proved correct. Sales were even below those of the previous month. Mr. Riley said something was going to have to be done and suggested that Mr. Bustamante himself make a field study of the situation. So Mr. Bustamante visited several stores. The store managers told him that they were too hard pressed financially to buy more Homar products, unless the company could make a special deal for them. Mr. Bustamante observed that this survey confirmed his opinion that all store owners were liars and would do anything they could to get good deals by playing one supplier against the other. The only thing to do was to keep up the pressure. Eventually they would have to break down and in the future they would think twice before loading up with competing items which did not have the same consumer appeal as Homar products.

He called in Mr. Leon and told him he was going to have to put more pressure on his salesmen. Mr. Leon repeated his doubts about the feasibility of getting results till Potter finished their promotion. He said he thought it would be better to use a large part of the salesmen's time in the next few weeks educating them on some new products that were going to come out soon and giving them some brush-up sessions on selling techniques. Mr. Bustamante told him emphatically that this was no time for salesmen to be in a classroom and told him, "Get out and get the men going." He then went directly to Mr. Riley and reported his conclusions and his opinion that they should fire Mr. Leon. He proposed that they bring in Mr. Marin, who was the top salesman in northern Mexico, to be the new submanager. Mr. Riley accepted his recommendation, and the next day the changes were ordered. Mr. Bustamante in private observed that he had known this was going to happen for some time. "Leon is just not the type for this job. I could see that from the beginning. He just doesn't understand selling. Imagine thinking about putting the men in a classroom at a time like this. Now Marin is taking over. He'll get sales going. He's a good salesman. He'll get after those salesmen and get out and sell himself if he has to. We are going to have a really good sales operation here again."

Which of the two men had the better plan of action in this situation can scarcely be determined from the data at hand. We would like to know, for example, how long Potter's promotion is going to last and how heavily the stores are stocked up. Getting this information might prove difficult, so a solution at best might have to be reached without it. The notable feature of the story, however, is the lack of interest in dealing with the problem on a factual basis. The essence of the comments in every conversation is the man's personal feel for the situation which is the result of a few triggering pieces of information and his emotional reactions to them. Mr. Bustamante hears that sales are down and his response is not a careful search for the reasons for the drop and a review of alternative strategies to meet it; it is to roll out the heavy guns of sales effort and advertising and bowl the enemy over. Mr. Leon is defeated and defensive and his response throughout is to do nothing.

When Mr. Bustamante's approach fails his feelings turn against Mr. Leon and, in the direct contradiction between his earlier confidence in Mr. Leon and his implication at the end that he always knew Mr. Leon would never be able to do the job, we have an actual distortion of facts. Then there is Mr. Bustamante's abounding confidence in Mr. Marin which has little apparent logical basis. Mr. Marin has been a good salesman, but as there is still no clear understanding of the character of the sales problem confronting the company and, since Mr. Marin has not been a manager, how can one have assurance that everything is going to be all right? Finally there is the interesting fact that no one has explored the possibility of a change in the discount. This may be perfectly sound, but if a competitor is adopting a tactic strong enough to have this sort of impact on sales, it is worth at least considering.

Mr. Riley's role in all of this is an interesting one. He was essentially passive. His attitude was that he did not have a good feel for Mexican marketing problems and that it was sound to delegate authority to Mr. Bustamante. He did not, however, ask for facts which he could have done without infringing on Mr. Bustamante's authority. He appeared at least in this respect to have adopted his associates' pattern of administration.

Here in the confused arena of daily action we can see the types of situations in which the analytical approach might be applied and the way the Mexican cultural tendencies respond in such situations. There is first the general tendency to act according to the emotions of the moment—to charge into more sales effort, to sit back and wait it out, et cetera. Then also there is the adherence to established rules or formulas for action, such as more advertising and maintaining discounts. And finally the *proyectismo* in Mr. Bustamante, seeing certain success in his first approach and then equally sure of Mr.

Marin as a solution, but in neither case really examining his plan against the realities of the problem.

Elsewhere in the world there are similarities and differences in cultural attitudes in these respects. The commonest characteristic is the respect for dogma and authority as the source of answers to problems. The authoritarian character of education found in Mexico is almost universal. The problem solving, individual-analysis approach is a relatively new movement which is only partially accepted in the United States and is developing slowly in other parts of the world. The emotion-thought-action differences in personalities vary notably among the peoples of the world. *Proyectismo* may not have a direct equivalent elsewhere but attitudes of a similar order are found in the varying capacities of individuals to gain satisfactions in dreams and contemplation of plans.

THE ACTION PHASE

If an artist were asked to portray the spirit of modern industrial management, he might do no more than draw a picture of a clock and a production scheduling board. Those two devices symbolize the management mind in action: the constant sense of the future and the need to plan, the compulsion to fulfill plans, and the obedience to obligations governed by accurately measured time. These are the attitudes which permit large numbers of specialists to work efficiently with a minimum of waste of resources. They are unquestionably a dominant element in the modern United States culture and, among United States business executives, they come as close to universal personality traits as any attitudes we have discussed so far.

The strength of these attitudes in the United States is the subject of much attention. Their value in furthering material productivity is generally conceded. But their value for the general well-being of men is widely questioned. Many people feel that they have usurped from man his power to control and enjoy his own destiny; that our people are now the slaves of the industrial machine they have created. It is certainly a valid question. All but the most insensitive people are conscious from time to time of the extent to which their individual interests and emotions are denied expression by the discipline of a society which places first importance on the demands of industrial productivity. The direction of time and effort are determined in a large portion of a man's activities by the requirements of effective performance on the job, which are in turn dictated by the planning and coordination necessary to keep the vast interdependent mechanisms of the United States economy going in something approaching smooth efficiency.

Whether the disciplines of the United States culture are in fact any more destructive of individual self-realization than those of other cultures is difficult to determine. In all cultures, the individual is restricted to some degree in order to assure effective group activity. Such disciplines as ethical codes, tribal customs, and class boundaries also limit individual self-realization and it is hard to weigh the set of disciplines of one society against another. A more important question is whether the United States culture will evolve into a pattern which allows a fuller degree of self-realization. This is a question which many thoughtful people are exploring today and we can hope that despite the pressures for material productivity in the new space age, the quest for fuller human satisfaction remains our highest priority.

These comments about the United States culture may appear as a digression from the problem of understanding the attitudes of the foreign executive. They are not, however, for their tenor reflects the point of view of many foreign people. Except in a few places, notably northern Europe, the cultural attitudes which govern men in the action phase of their work are quite different from those of the United States culture. Furthermore, there tends to be a definite aversion to the standards of the United States culture in this respect, something which is not true of other cultural differences which we have discussed. The United States patterns of democracy, inventiveness and scientific analysis are generally admired. But the disciplines which govern the way we go about our daily work are held in low repute. A large portion of those foreigners who have passed the point of believing that the United States teems with gangsters and marauding Indians, visualize the typical United States citizen as driven through life by the demands of his job and standardized patterns of mass-produced leisure, with no time or capacity for finding individual enjoyment in life. This characterization is extreme, like most stereotypes, but it points up the contrasts with foreign cultures which are important in understanding foreign executives.

The United States executive overseas is constantly confronted by problems which originate in these contrasts. He finds that people are often late for appointments, that they do not plan well, that when plans are made they do not stick to them, and so forth. Sometimes these problems are due to other attitudes which we have already discussed. For example, a subordinate who does not carry out a plan to which he had verbally agreed may actually never have intended to carry it out, giving the verbal agreement simply to placate the boss. But in a great many cases, the problem lies in the basic attitudes of the individual toward the action phase of work. To understand these attitudes we need to examine them against the setting of history and environment. For this purpose Mexico again serves as a useful case.

The key to understanding attitudes toward accomplishment of work is an appreciation of what is important to the individual. In Mexico, very few people are actively opposed to being on time, following plans, or obeying any of the other rules of industrial discipline. When they do not obey them, it is because some conflicting avenue of action appeared and they felt it was more important. While quite a variety of conflicting avenues may arise, two stand out in Mexico as the most important: the expression of personal inclinations and the maintenance of personal alliances.

The importance of expressing personal inclinations is related to the attitudes of the man of passion which were discussed in the preceding section. The problems it presents in the action phase of a man's work are illustrated by the experience of the Taylor Pharmaceutical Company.

The Taylor Company made an arrangement in November, 1946, with Gonzales and Company whereby Taylor received a 25 per cent interest in the Mexican firm in return for the rights to the manufacture and sale of Taylor products in Mexico. A program of expansion and capital increases was laid out for Gonzales and Company. The Mexican company would start making one Taylor product after another over an extended period and new facilities would be added as needed. The timing of this evolution was geared to the expected rate of acquisition of skills by the Gonzales personnel in handling the complex Taylor manufacturing processes.

The main figures in negotiating this agreement were Walter Warren, Taylor's Vice President for Foreign Operations, and Manuel Gonzales, President of Gonzales and Company. Mr. Warren was a chemical engineer. He was generally considered a very competent and efficient administrator on the basis of his career in working up to the top of the Taylor production organization. Mr. Gonzales was the son of Romero Gonzales, who had founded Gonzales and Company in

1928. The Gonzales family were quite wealthy, owning several other factories. Romero Gonzales had devoted full time to the drug business, while his brothers managed the other factories. In 1943 he died suddenly, leaving the business to his only son, Manuel, who was twenty-five. Manuel was an intelligent and energetic young man and he approached his job with the zeal of a missionary. He felt that he had an obligation to his father to build up the concern which had been the focus of his life. Manuel owned half of the stock in the company, and the remainder was divided between his two uncles. The latter, however, did not participate actively in the business.

The initial agreement provided that manufacture of a few of the simplest Taylor products would start as soon as possible. Ten million pesos of new capital to construct facilities would be provided pro rata by the stockholders. Plans for the new facilities were developed in detail and in April, 1947, construction started, with two Taylor engineers supervising the work. Almost immediately Mr. Gonzales requested that Taylor approve additional construction involving production of certain products which were not included in the initial program. Mr. Warren responded in the negative, making clear that Taylor would approve no additional programs until the current plan was completed and the operations were satisfactory.

There were a few further difficulties in the following months and then in late August, Taylor was informed by its bank in Mexico City that 800,000 pesos had been paid out to Mr. Gonzales against his statement that Taylor had obligated itself for that amount. Mr. Warren flew to Mexico City immediately and found that Mr. Gonzales had told the bank that the promise in the original agreement for a long-range expansion plan and the capital to finance it, permitted him to draw on Taylor for its share of such additional capital at anytime he needed it. This was entirely contrary to Mr. Warren's understanding of the agreement. Mr. Warren went immediately to Mr. Gonzales and told him he had acted in bad faith in the matter. Mr. Gonzales expressed great unhappiness and explained that the company was in debt and in danger of becoming bankrupt unless it had the additional money. It was apparent to Mr. Warren that the company was indeed in difficult financial straits because Mr. Gonzales was pushing ahead on various schemes for expansion. Though technically Taylor could sue Gonzales, that would not remedy the financial situation. So Mr. Warren limited himself to a stern lecture to Mr. Gonzales on responsible conduct. Mr. Gonzales appeared quite contrite over his actions and promised Mr. Warren that he would do nothing like this again without consulting him.

Nevertheless, further disturbing incidents continued to be reported by Taylor's engineers and lawyer in Mexico, and in September Mr. Warren learned that a new warehouse was being constructed and a generator had been bought. These facilities were not in the initial plan and would cost 300,000 pesos. The company lawyer was asked to investigate and he found that Mr. Gonzales had used funds which were allocated for the main construction program. He also discovered that Mr. Gonzales had signed commitments for a further major construction program which would cost 13,000,000 pesos. Mr. Warren flew immediately to Mexico and spoke very firmly with Mr. Gonzales about his headstrong actions and irresponsibility. Mr. Gonzales admitted that he had not acted properly and assured Mr. Warren that he would change his ways. He pointed out, however, that the company's business was growing and that it was financially hard pressed, so that additional capital was essential to keep it solvent. Mr. Warren could see that this was true and agreed to supply further capital, emphasizing as he did so that this was the last increase that would be allowed until the main construction activities were in operation and their efficiency established.

For a brief while Mr. Gonzales appeared to be meeting Mr. Warren's desires. Then further problems arose, resulting in irritations on both sides and eventually culminating in a complete break in relations between Taylor and Mr. Gonzales, who was supported by his two uncles. By this time the company had become so indebted to a bank that Taylor was able to control the situation. They took over management of the company, and Mr. Gonzales was removed.

While several attitudes are relevant to the problems in this case, the aspects which apply to the present discussion are the differences in the points of view of the two men toward the plans which had been made. To Mr. Warren they were firm blueprints which had to be adhered to in order that financial resources, personnel training, and all the other pieces of the industrial machine should develop in an orderly and effective sequence. To Mr. Gonzales, the plans were subordinate to his own urges, which in this case were to build the business as rapidly as possible. Behind these differences were the basic attitudes of the men: Mr. Warren instinctively obedient to "the plan" and "the agreement," things which in his life were the standards of proper performance; and Mr. Gonzales, instinctively responsive to his personal inclinations, the expression of which meant by his standards the fulfillment of life. It happens in this situation that Mr. Gonzales has the instincts of a business promoter and it may be that his deviations from the plan were sound in a business sense. But the standard of performance derived from the culture is unpredictable because it in itself is not concerned with business. For example, an executive may become thoroughly absorbed in a discussion of politics at lunch and not show up for an important business conference in the afternoon. Or he may become so excited about a conflict with another executive that he neglects a report which he is supposed to submit on a proposed change in the production layout.

The second standard, the maintenance of personal relationships, may conflict both with the concepts of disciplined execution of work and with the desire for self-expression. But in the traditional Mexican system, the alliances which a man develops are considered essential to success and, when they make demands upon him, they take precedence. Among the executives observed in this study, important conflicts between these standards did not usually appear. For the most part the problem was simply one of time. While there were substantial variations among the men, a considerable amount of time was typically spent in substantively unproductive conversation with others, particularly bankers, suppliers and similar crucial outside contacts. Expenditure of time in this way is, of course, common also in the United States. The difference was, therefore, only one of degree and not very measurable at that. Furthermore, the Mexican society being as it is, it is in the best interests of a company that its executives devote considerable time to maintaining good relations with key contacts spread through industry and government.

In some cases, however, situations arise in which the demands of maintenance of personal relationships conflict with specific obligations of management efficiency as conceived by United States executives. This was the case in the story at the start of the book. Harry Grey felt that reduction of costs required putting pressure on the supplier, Ramex, to give better service, or getting a new supplier. Pedro Gomez felt it essential to keep Carlos, the sales manager of Ramex, as a friend and ally. In this case it is highly debatable which is actually right from a straight business point of view. Pedro Gomez is adhering to his position because it is part of his personality. It is something in which he believes deeply. He has not apparently made an attempt to analyze his position critically in the light of the facts that Harry Grey has explored about other suppliers and the experience of other companies. But, though his belief is blind, it still may be valid. The structure of Mexican industry may be such that the company is wiser to stick with a supplier who does not give perfect service, but with whom they have, through Pedro and Carlos, a tie which assures at least minimum performance.

The cultural attitudes which affect approaches to action are natural outgrowths of the conditions under which the people have lived. Looking at the development of the United States and Mexico we find an interesting contrast in the experiences of the people in the action phase of life. The United States has for the most part always been a land of abundant resources and independent producers. Individual effort was rewarded in the beginning by survival and later by material benefits. If a man cleared more land, he grew more crops. If he endured the hardships of the trail, he found land or perhaps mineral wealth in the West. It all depended on him. Others might join with him in collective defense or productive effort, but always the work of the individual was clearly evident as the gauge of his value to the group. Reinforcing the individualism[10] of the pioneer were the attitudes which are summed up in the expression, "the Protestant Ethic," which came out of the Reformation and industrial revolution in Europe, setting up hard work as a religiously-approved code. From this background developed the United States attitude that it is of first importance to adhere industriously and consistently to a tangibly productive purpose.

In Mexico, the story was different. The land was poorer and it was already quite thickly populated by Indians when the Spanish arrived. The original settlers were generally from higher social classes than those who went to North America, and they did not usually do their own work. Rather, they enslaved or impressed the Indians to perform their physical labor. The standards of a man's success were the number of servants he could command and the amount of leisure he could afford. Since both land and slaves were limited and the strongest agent for redistributing them was the government, a man's most productive effort was the development of allies who could help him to get more in return for some favor. Meantime, among the lower classes there was a limit to the amount of physical effort which seemed worthwhile.

---

[10] The difference between this individualism and the individualistic personality is discussed in Appendix B.

With land scarce, it availed little to toil harder, so people found their satisfaction in what pleasures their inclinations suggested, whether it be dozing in the sun, or cockfighting, or making artistic creations.

Supplementing these structural elements were, of course, the character of the people and the failure of the concepts of the Protestant Ethic to touch Spain. Out of all of these forces developed a pattern of life which is evident in the cultural attitudes of today. Satisfactions for both the rich and the poor lay in the expression of personal inclinations. Work was a necessity, something to be done by those who were obligated to do it, and not a standard of success or a form of personal fulfillment. And the pattern of personal alliances which a man could develop was a major determinant for his success.

Related to this subject are the cultural attitudes toward time, a question about which there is considerable confusion. People frequently say glibly that the Mexicans have no sense of time. That may be true of the Indians in the villages. It is possible that many of them live completely in the present, with little contemplation of the future or the ordering of their lives in relation to time. But it is not true of the urban middle and upper classes. They are clearly conscious of the time factor in life and think much about the future.

There is something different, however, between the effect of time in the cultural attitudes of the United States and Mexico. One cannot live in Mexico without realizing that. The difference seems to be of the same character as the conflict between discipline and expression of personal inclinations discussed above. The United States cultural attitudes are epitomized in Benjamin Franklin's adage, "Time is money." Time is a tangible resource to be ordered and then obeyed just like all of the other segments of the industrial scheme. In the Mexican culture time is a part of the substance of life in which one expresses oneself. It must be considered and utilized, if life is to be lived fully; but it, along with the other ordering disciplines, is resisted in their interference with the more important experiences of life.

This is the fundamental attitude toward time in relation to work. The question of planning for the future is related to it, but it is a special problem. A quick survey of the plans which abound in Mexican history and the elaborate programs which lie behind the tremendous current growth of Mexico is sufficient proof that the minds of many Mexicans are very much in the future. We have already noted in the concept of *proyectismo*, however, that there is a tendency to avoid analytical toughness in developing plans. The concept of the future is part of this story. Historically, as we have seen, plans in Mexico have failed with great frequency. The future for the Mexican is therefore a very uncertain thing. This has led to a cultural tendency to avoid completeness and precision in planning for the future. There is much concocting of schemes, but it is very hard to get a firm schedule of appointments for next week.

Summing up these cultural attitudes toward action, we see an individual for whom the accepted pattern of life is the fullest possible expression of personal inclinations, but with necessary attention to preserving the structure of alliances which sustain his position. The requirements of disciplined management action stand apart from this pattern. Increasingly, they must be accepted as prerequisites for material advancement in life, and they appear to be finding more and more actual acceptance in the personal attitudes of executives. On balance, however, the pressures of the culture are set against them.

The United States executive is likely to find much this same picture in other foreign countries. As I noted at the start of this section, the drive and discipline of the United States culture are generally deplored by other peoples. Their pace of life has been slower and efforts for material productivity having provided little reward, the people have given greater attention to finding expression for various aspects of their personalities. Currently, however, the demands of industrial expansion are severely testing these cultures. People are finding that greater material wealth requires greater discipline in action at the expense of other values. The business executive, along with the industrial laborer, is more and more dominated by the impersonal, compelling rhythm of the factory. Recognizing the shortcomings of our own society in providing full satisfactions for our people, we may wish the peoples of other lands well in their quest for a new cultural formula. Those who respect the finer qualities of foreign cultures are disturbed to find the demands of industrial productivity weakening them and hope sincerely that they may, at least in part, be retained in the new patterns now evolving. There is little, however, that we can actually do, as it is the basic evolution within each country and not the influence of a handful of United States executives which will determine the character of the new culture. Meantime, the United States executive lives with the situation as it is—typically a culture to some degree antithetical to the demands of effective management action but with individual executives possessing to varying degrees the capacity for orderly and disciplined execution of work.

SUMMARY

In this chapter we have considered the three main phases of the process of accomplishing work—innovation, analysis and action. Throughout, a model has been assumed as the standard for high industrial productivity—the executive with a searching, creative mind, with sharp analytical capacities, and with a disciplined and persistent approach to the execution of plans. Through a combination of circumstances, this standard has to a large degree been achieved in the United States. In other cultures, however, lacking similar circumstances, one or more of the basic ingredients is often lacking. Creativity and innovation have been fostered in some areas, while in others conformity has been the established pattern of life. Intellectual and analytical approaches to action are instinctive among some peoples, but for others obedience to impulse or tradition are natural. Finally, in most cultures the discipline of industrial activity is not highly regarded, the people acting out their lives with more concern for their immediate feelings and the development of personal relationships.

Chapter 4

Motivations

The goals which men set for themselves and the intensity with which they pursue those goals have much to do with the character of their work and the administrative frameworks which are suitable for their effective performance. An understanding of differences in motivations is therefore important to the United States executive seeking satisfactory relations with executives of other nations. In this endeavor he is aided to some degree by an awareness of the differences in motivations which abound in the United States society. Even our industrial culture contains within itself a fair range of motivational patterns, not just as deviations from a basic norm, but as the standards of large groups. For example, scientific personnel generally have objectives in the independent search for the satisfactions of discovery which are far less common among the professional managerial class.

In his experiences abroad, however, the United States executive finds quite different types of motivational variations. Most important, he frequently finds that the motivations of his immediate associates in the management group are different from his own, whereas in the United States he was accustomed to a widely-accepted common standard of motivations among his close associates. The objective in this chapter is to spell out the character of these differences among the men who are found in professional management jobs in foreign countries.

There are two main dimensions to the motivation question. One is the character dimension, the nature of the objectives of a man, which set the direction for his efforts. The other is the dynamic dimension, which is a measure of the force which the motivations exert on the individual and the energy with which he seeks his ends. It is, of course, the combination of these two dimensions which determines the actions of the individual; but, for analytical purposes, it is helpful to approach them separately.

Common to the analysis of both dimensions is the weight of culture in shaping the motivations of men. The national ideology plays a major role in this aspect of a man's personality because the search for approval from others is a key factor in determining the character of a man's goals. Likewise the channels of progress which society opens to him delineate the types of goals a man may reasonably select and the ways in which he may strive for their accomplishment. Thus the analysis will be cast very largely in terms of cultural patterns of motivations and their background in foreign environments.

The Character of Motivations

Discussing the nature of men's motivations is not easy. We cannot polarize the differences among them because, except in rare instances, several types of motivations are important in the character of each individual and the range of combinations of these types is perplexing in its variety. One frequently hears sweeping characterizations of Americans as materialists and some foreign peoples as motivated by the satisfaction of aesthetic or spiritual urges. These generalizations may provide some helpful perspective, but as guides to understanding differences among the executives of different nations they can be grossly misleading. I shall not attempt, therefore, to describe composite motivational patterns of foreign executives. Rather, it seems most useful to discuss the chief types of motivations and the significance of each in foreign cultures. From this discussion the United States executive may then draw ideas to apply in whatever combination is suitable to the foreign executives he meets.

Several types of motivations are significant to men in administrative jobs: material gain, power, social satisfaction and interest in work. Motivational patterns combining these elements are a vital part of the United States ideology. It is generally expected that United States executives seek substantial material gain and power, that they will find satisfaction in the fraternal aspects of their work and in the high social status accorded the businessman, and that the challenges of their work will absorb and satisfy them. While we recognize numerous exceptions and variations within this framework, it is reasonaby accurate and useful as a starting point for understanding the motivations of executives in the United States.

Abroad, the motivations of executives fall in the same general areas, but they usually assume a different character. That is, the material benefits of a job, the power and social position it affords, and the satisfactions which the work itself provides are all significant to foreign executives. However, the types of results in each area which the foreign executive finds rewarding are often significantly different from the United States pattern. In the preceding chapters we have already seen some of these differences because motivations have been in the background of the personality characteristics we have discussed. Chapter Two covered a major portion of the power and social satisfaction side of the individual's motivations. For the individualistic personality the development of a strong tactical position in relation to other people is the prime objective. Power for itself does not appear to be as important, but power is a common objective because it strengthens the position of the individual. The fraternal satisfaction of working with others may be enjoyed by the individualistic personality, but it was evident throughout Chapter Two that it was a minor factor in the evolution of the executive's relationships.

For the group-oriented personality the fraternal satisfactions are primary, with the quest for power playing a secondary role. For this type of executive congenial relations with associates at work are essential. He wants to be liked and accepted by the men around him and to feel he is a part of a group activity. Within the group he may find satisfaction in exercising a degree of leadership and authority. In this form power is part of his motivational pattern, but it is subordinate to the achievement of friendly relations with members of the group.

In Chapter Three, three sides of the satisfactions the individual derives from the work he performs were evident. First, there was the discussion of innovation from which it developed that in some cultures there is a general drive for creativity and in some there is not. Thus it appears generally true of executives in some countries that the development of new ideas and methods is a strong working motivation, while in other countries it is absent or at least not an important force.

Second, behind the variations in analytical performance of executives, we saw that there were cultural differences in the satisfactions men found in thinking and analyzing. Among some peoples intensive mental activity is enjoyed for itself. For others, however, there is little satisfaction in thinking through problems and ideas. Some of them may accept analysis as valuable for a further end, the Anglo-American, action-oriented man finding that action is more effective if it is pre-analyzed. By others, however, it may be disliked because it hampers achievement of more valued objectives, the Latin emotion-oriented man avoiding analysis because it inhibits the expression of feelings.

Third, in the action phase men show different patterns of motivation. Out of the Anglo-Saxon culture and the Protestant Ethic has come a compulsive drive to disciplined action which motivates men in carrying out their work. Such men respect as fundamental to proper conduct obedience to plans and systems developed to accomplish specified objectives. In some other cultures, these disciplining codes are essentially lacking, and in their absence the individual in action is motivated by either the emotions of the moment or his understanding of what is generally regarded as appropriate action for a given situation according to the traditions of his society.

While these characteristics describe a major portion of the motivational patterns of executives, two other pieces must be fitted in to complete the picture of the main forces which direct the interests and energies of an executive at work. First, there is the question of material gain, and then the problem of social status.

Material Gain

One of the great myths of our times is that material gain is less important as a motivation overseas than in the United States. Like all myths, this one has its core of truth. The United States has been relatively wealthy in material terms and its people have been so absorbed with material production that they have given less importance to some other satisfactions. By contrast, in vast areas of the world economic standards of living have been low and have provided scant comfort for most individuals. The people have tended to find their satisfactions in other directions: in aesthetic pleasure, in social activities, and in religious contemplation. Thus it is true that material rewards play a smaller part in most foreign cultures.

But this is not the same thing as saying that material gain is less important as a motivation. To the contrary, it appears that material advancement is extremely important in most foreign cultures today.

Viewing the situation broadly, we can see this motive manifest in the drive for economic development and the appeals of Communism. In the narrower sphere of business life, it was strikingly evident throughout my research. On the whole it appeared that salaries and other material rewards were, if anything, more important to the foreign executives than to their United States counterparts. This was evident in comments about their earnings and their financial problems. It also showed up in expressions of envy at United States executives and the United States in general. The sense of discrimination which will be discussed in Chapter Six accounted in part for these feelings. Foreign executives generally feel that companies, in paying United States executives more, imply that the foreigners are inferior. But, living and working with a group of foreign executives, one cannot escape the fact that they value in itself the greater range of material benefits which the United States economy provides.

Their feelings are relatively easy to understand, if we look at the way of life of executives in a country like Mexico by comparison with that of executives in the United States. There are a few rich people in Mexico who from their own resources can buy practically anything they want. These people usually have their own businesses, however, and are not found in the professional management group who work for United States companies.

The professional executives are mostly drawn from the middle class. Their own resources are quite limited and their standard of living is set by current earnings. Their salaries are such that by the standards of their country they live very well, but it is still a relatively tight existence in which a little bigger paycheck can make a significant difference. By contrast a comparable executive in the United States usually has a fuller complement of material possessions and a small increase in salary will not benefit him as much, especially as he will lose a larger share of it to the tax collector.

For example, we may compare two men recently promoted to the position of sales manager, one in Mexico and the other in the United States, their jobs being roughly equal in level of responsibility. The Mexican is able to afford a comfortable but quite small house with a minute lawn. His promotion to sales manager meant that at last he could afford a second hand car, which is squeezed into his tiny garage. He bought a television set on the installment plan a year ago and keeping up the payments on it and the car is taking all of his excess income. In order to give his children a good education, he is sending them to a private school. He has two servants who, under the direction of his wife, take care of the house. The United States sales manager has a good-sized house in a suburb, with an ample yard and a two car garage. He has a house full of mechanical and electrical devices and there is a car he bought new last year in the garage. His children are going to a good public school. Financially he is living close to his income but the promotion to sales manager has given him some excess and he is currently debating with his wife whether to spend it on a second car to make their life easier or to save it for higher education for the children.

The average United States executive worrying about a pile of bills and the requests of his wife and children may think this a dubious comparison. He may see his life as financially hard pressed and a raise as a vital matter. This is doubtless true and it underscores the fact that the motivation of material gain is important in the United States culture. But stepping back from his own position, the United States executive may appreciate that there is a difference in the case of the foreigner. The Mexican sales manager is much closer to the position of, for example, a top office clerk or skilled craftsman in the United States society. These people are striving for and hopeful of a quite full way of life for themselves and their children. They can just barely afford many comforts. Those they have are precious accomplishments to be guarded assiduously, and the new steps ahead from the next salary rise are awaited anxiously. That is how the foreign executive typically feels. He is acutely conscious of the sea of poverty which envelops the masses in all but a very few countries. He appreciates deeply the benefits which material goods bring him and he is eager for more of them.

A special aspect of this subject is the search for security. The urge to assure one's future material welfare is doubtless common to all societies. It appears, however, that it is a special problem with foreign executives. In interviews with Mexican executives, concern about the future cropped up frequently, even in quite young men. A man in his early forties, for example, felt that the important incentives to stay with the company were "a sense of security and good pay right now." In elaborating on the first, which he felt was most important, he observed, "Men want to feel that the company will look after them. They want to feel that they won't be discarded when they get old and are not quite so useful to the company."

The reasons for this concern about security lie in the nature of the society and the changes now taking place. Security for the older members of societies is generally institutionalized. That is, it is established along some set pattern. In the United States today various payment systems, notably social security and private pensions, are recognized as the normal way through which people are taken care of as they pass beyond productively self-supporting years. While each individual has his problems and worries, broadly this system is effective and accepted.

In Mexico, as in most countries, the institutional system has been either the family or the paternalistic employer or both. When the Mexican could no longer support himself, he expected in most instances that his sons would take care of him. As traditionally the eldest son and perhaps other children had continued to live in the father's house and contribute earnings to the household, this transfer of responsibility was quite easy. The employer usually had a lesser role, but for workers in company housing, and especially for peons on the haciendas, the employer would continue to provide a degree of protection and support. Thus there was a national tradition of the employer as a supplement to the security system of the family, even though for men of the executive level the actual role of the employer was minor.

Now changes in the social structure of the country are breaking up the family security system. Mr. Mendez, an older executive, who was deeply worried about his future, summed up the situation, "I can't seem to save anything for retirement. Costs are high, especially with two children going through college. It used to be that the children took care of their parents. But that is passing. They will get married and then they'll have their own children and they can't afford to help me. I'll have to take care of myself. But it is extremely hard to save." The children have gone out of the family physically, often moving to other cities, and the concept of the financially independent small family unit is gaining ground. This same change accompanied urbanization and industrialization in the United States. The similarity of current trends throughout the world suggests that it is inevitable as the economic revolution proceeds. In any case, men like Mr. Mendez feel it in their own lives and it arouses in them a gnawing sense of insecurity. The old system is clearly crumbling but there is no new system to fill the gap. What is a man to do?

In due course a system of financial security will doubtless evolve in Mexico. Under Mexican law, companies are already required to give a man upon retirement a lump sum equal to his pay for three months plus twenty days for every year of service. For workers in some industries there is also a retirement pension scheme managed by the social security system. Few Mexican companies have executive pension systems, however, so for the professional managerial class retirement income largely depends upon what they can save from what we have already seen is a hard-pressed current budget. The problem is the same in United States companies which do not generally extend their pension systems to foreign executives, a subject which will be discussed in Chapter Six.

This is the problem of security at the end of a man's working days. Immediate job security is another type of problem but no less significant in some countries. In Mexico it is not a major concern of the executives. None of the men I interviewed spoke of it as a problem for themselves or others. This is not surprising. Mexico is in the midst of an explosive economic boom in which competent manpower rivals capital as a limiting factor. There is no appreciable unemployment of educated men capable of doing management work. Therefore, a man need have no real worry about current job security.

The shortage of educated personnel prevails in many foreign countries. In a few cases, however, the story is different, the most notable instance being India. It is estimated that there were half a million unemployed college graduates in India in 1956. The country's educational system and economic needs are far out of line. The former was geared up to provide a large flow of candidates for the British colonial government and, in a society which places high value on learning, every young man who could possibly afford it has sought a university degree. The output of university graduates has been very high and many of them are ill-equipped for management jobs because their training was for government service. At the same time economic development has been held to a snail's pace by limited capital and the tremendous size of the country's problems. So few jobs open up each year, men find it hard to obtain positions, and holding on to one when it is found is a major preoccupation.

We find, therefore, that material gain is a significant objective in foreign cultures, manifesting itself variously in concern for current income, for short-term job security, and for security at the end of the working career. Because of the difficulty of achieving these objectives with the limited economic resources available, many foreign ideologies do encourage the individual to seek satisfaction in other intellectual or emotional ways. But the urge to material betterment is present none the less, especially in the type of man who becomes an executive in a country in which the promise of economic progress is the rallying cry of the day.

Social Status

Man, being a social animal, is motivated by the search for satisfactions in relations with other people. That far we may go in a universal generalization. Beyond it lie a variety of social systems, each with its own arrangement of roles and rewards, a map for social living, as it were, which the individual follows in his search for social satisfaction.

For the business executive the map has symbols which describe his relations with people outside the company and with those inside the small social world of his own organization. Depending on his personality, he may ignore or misunderstand the symbols but, unless he is extremely resistant, they are a strong influence on him.

The earlier discussion of the character of men's attitudes toward fraternal satisfactions and power covered a major portion of the field of social objectives. For most men, these motivations seem the strongest forces in their relations with their immediate associates. A further element, social status, is significant in these relations, however, and it is of great importance in a man's broader objectives in his relations with society as a whole.

One element in the earlier discussion provides a useful take-off point for considering the social status attitudes of men in different cultures. The individualistic executive is conscious of being among a society of men and relates himself to them in a competitive manner, gaining status at the expense of others. The group-oriented individual wants to be accepted by the group and gains fraternal satisfactions from his activities in conjunction with them. In the former, the objective is one of social differentiation; in the latter, social differentiation is minimized. This difference carries through into other personal attitudes. The essence of several thought-provoking analyses of the United States culture is that the avoidance of differentiation and the quest for uniformity is the modern ideological standard.[1] In brief, people feel they should be like other people in order to be approved of and

[1] For example, Erich Fromm, *Sane Society* (New York: Rinehart, 1955) and William H. Whyte, *The Organization Man* (New York: Simon and Schuster, 1956).

accepted into social groups, and the competitive drive is going out of the culture. This conclusion may be too extreme. The broad distinction is valid, however, and the idea of social differentiation is a good starting point for understanding other variations in social objectives because it is in the background of most of them.

Differentiation in varying intensities is basic to men's social goals in most countries because great importance is attached to the segments into which society is divided. Some social stations are considered high and some low, and men generally strive for the high ones. There are several bases for social differentiation, including intellectual accomplishment, religious position and racial background. While each has some relevance in business, two stand out as most important, and the analysis will therefore be limited to them. They are economic level and professional status.

Economic Level

In all societies one finds people who are labeled as upper, middle, and lower classes. The meaning of these distinctions varies greatly from country to country, however. In some, notably the Scandinavian and Anglo-Saxon countries, the span between the bottom and top of the economic scale is far less than in the great areas of the world which suffer from deep economic poverty. Where there are major differences between classes in actual economic welfare, there is also a tendency to attach social consequence to one's economic status. In Mexico, the span between economic classes is not so wide as in Asia, most of Africa, and the Middle East. Still it is great enough so that the social implications of economic level are strongly felt.

The wealthy at the top of the economic scale have a commanding social position. Their wealth gives them power and primary social rights which, in a country with an individualistic culture, they use quite fully for personal advantage. Their sense of superior position is strikingly evident in the arrogant disregard for the law which many of them show and the dominance which they assume in social relations.

For the middle class the important fact is that they are above the masses. This is a major social distinction in their minds and they protect it jealously. In my observations of middle-class Mexican executives, this distinction was noted as one of just a few points which were the source of very intense emotion. For example, one of the symbols of their status is that wives do not work. The author was entertained one night in the home of an executive and, enjoying a piece of cake, re-marked unthinkingly to the hostess, "You certainly baked a fine cake." The husband immediately snapped out, "In Mexico our wives do not do the cooking." On another occasion a young executive who had worked in the United States for a while became quite flustered as he explained how he had been forced to wash dishes to make a living. "You know, when a boy is from the middle class in Mexico he just doesn't wash dishes."

The lower classes are another world to both the upper and middle classes, so much so that I have on occasion had a lengthy conversation in which the attitudes of "The Mexicans" on such matters as politics were discussed and it was quite evident that the Mexican in question was completely ignoring the lower-class point of view. When he said, "The Mexicans feel——" he was referring to those with means and education and the rest just were not part of his consciousness. One side effect of this state of mind explains something which often concerns people from the United States. United States executives and others traveling overseas are commonly depressed by the extreme and ever-present poverty. It creates in many an uncomfortable feeling of guilt that they should have so much while others live a miserable existence. They then wonder how the local people who are well off materially can tolerate the conditions around them with peace of mind. The answer lies in this detached attitude of the upper and middle classes. To them it is another part of the world and therefore no more de-pressing than it is to the United States executive back in his living room in New York. They are quite conscious of poverty as a fact and of the lower classes as segments of society of which they are happy not to be members, but they do not have any empathy or feeling for the thoughts and attitudes of people at that level.

The Mexican lower classes themselves are aware that they are at the bottom of the heap. They expect to be ordered around, to act sub-servient, and in general to do the dirty work of society and get very little in return for it. They may not in the process lose their integrity as persons, but so far as social status is concerned, they know that they do not count for much. There is no pride in being a common man as such or in having risen from the masses, as there is in the United States ideology. Sometimes a man does rise into a higher class, but if he does, he tries to forget and hide his origins, for they are no asset except pos-sibly in politics, and they are clearly a social handicap.

This economic classification affects men in various ways. It is, of course, tied to the search for material gain. It is obvious to all executives that financial advancement means not only more material goods but an advance in social position as well. It also results in a general tendency to emphasize the prerogatives of status within the company. For example, in one instance observed in this study men above a certain level systematically came to work at least an hour late and worked a comparable period overtime in the evening. Titles were the source of frequent concern, an area involving both economic level and the subject of professional status covered in the next section. One man discussed at some length the question of which title would appear superior: production superintendent or superintendent of production. In another company, as a result of a poorly conceived earlier organization plan, one of the Mexicans had been designated as regional sales director. This man was responsible for several field salesmen and in the usual company parlance he should have been called a regional supervisor. However, the old title had been retained because the management knew it meant a great deal to the man, and, if it were changed, those with whom he worked, both salesmen and customers, would interpret it as a demotion, which would be a hard blow for him. Likewise such symbols of status as a private office and a secretary loomed large in men's thinking. One company earned at least a part of the strong loyalty of its executives by allowing each to select the furnishings for his own office. Such symbols are, of course, a major element in the psychology of United States executives. In Mexico, however, they appear more important and in relations with United States executives they assume still a greater significance because of the problems of sensitivity and pride which are discussed in Chapter Six. If he is not careful, a United States executive can easily threaten some symbol of the foreign executive's social status and in doing so aggravate sensitivities which are easily aroused.

In his daily work, the sense of social status along economic lines may affect a man because the capacity to perform various jobs is dependent on social motivations and the ability to deal effectively with relationships which cross social boundaries. For example, a sales manager with a middle-class background may need to develop close relations with wealthy factory owners in order to sell his products. Or a man may have to assume the character of a new social status, as in the case of a worker promoted up from the ranks to a supervisory position in a plant. The problems of such men are not strange to the

United States, but we do not count them as a major obstacle. United States industry is geared to the concept of an all-purpose individual who is socially interchangeable—who can with equal ease sip a cocktail on Park Avenue and down a beer on the waterfront. Few probably have such flexibility, but the average executive has enough of it to adjust with tolerable ease to a variety of social settings.

Not so in Mexico nor in most other societies which have sharp social stratifications. United States and foreign executives interviewed in this research were in general agreement that the sense of social status set absolute limits on what a Mexican executive could do, and they felt that adjustments even within those limits were quite difficult. As one limit, they felt that only a rare middle-class or upper-class Mexican would be willing to do work which appeared to put him in an inferior status. They did not, therefore, assign college graduates to sales work for training, as is common in the United States, nor did they put young engineers out on the production line to "learn it the hard way."

As a sign of the changing times, there is not the complete unwillingness to do manual work which used to prevail and is still the rule in some other cultures. Production executives observed in this study were frequently willing to roll up their sleeves and pitch in on assembling new machinery or making repairs when their subordinates needed help. This shift is largely due to an evolution in standards of social practice within the confines of individual organizations. It is generally true that a man's social motivations are derived from the social group with whom he lives and from whom he seeks approval. When a Mexican is exposed to society in general as, for example, a salesman peddling his goods from customer to customer, he is sensitive to the standards of the country as a whole. But within the company in such matters as production work the standard is to a fair degree set by the company organization itself. Most United States subsidiaries have gone through an initial period when several United States engineers were around getting their hands dirty starting up machinery, and other executives, either on permanent assignment or temporary visits, have followed the same pattern. Also, Mexican engineers have usually had periods of training in United States plants. Out of these experiences has come an increasingly accepted view that it is all right for production executives to tackle jobs alongside their workers. This attitude extends, however, only to temporary expedients in the interests of good production. For a well-bred young man to don a pair of overalls and work eight hours a day on an assembly line would be quite another matter.

So much for the problems of flexibility moving downward on the social scale. Looking in the other direction, most executives felt the limits to upward flexibility were slightly less rigid but not much so. Mr. Raines, a typical United States executive, felt it would be quite impossible for a man from the lower classes to be a production manager. He also suspected that he would never be able to have a Mexican sales manager. His line of business required selling on a large lot basis to important Mexican businessmen who were of the upper class. He could not afford to hire a Mexican of similar status as sales manager and the middle-class executives he had would not, he felt, be able to carry on effective sales relations with the upper-class customers. A United States executive, though also of middle-class background, was generally accepted by the upper-class Mexicans. This line of reasoning fitted with the observations of other executives and was confirmed by some reports of failures of Mexicans who had been moved into sales jobs beyond their social capacities. In fact, however, two years after this interview, Mr. Raines did move a middle-class Mexican into the sales manager's spot, and there were indications that he was working out quite well. This incident does not prove the consensus to be unsound. It does indicate, however, that there is a degree of flexibility on the top side of the social scale.

These problems of social motivation and flexibility are common to all countries in the world. The relatively greater mobility and general economic leveling in the United States have reduced their significance in our society. The same general trend is apparent in most other countries. As yet, however, the process is not far advanced in most cases so a man's station in the economic hierarchy is of great importance to his social position.

Professional Status

A hierarchy based on skills exists in most societies as something more or less distinct from the economic scale, though often status in the one contributes to status in the other. The character of these hierarchies differs from culture to culture, first importance being given to those with such varied qualities as superior intellect, maximum physical strength, and knowledge of magic. The hierarchies encountered by the executive overseas do not show such a wide range, but they do differ from that in the United States, both in the status accorded to people with various skills and the significance attached to their status. In Mexico both types of differences may be readily observed.

Within the middle- and upper-class levels of Mexican society from which most executives are drawn, professional status is as important a measure of social distinction as economic level. Professions are rated in a hierarchy and where a man's work places him on this scale usually goes far in determining his social standing. At the top of the hierarchy are the lawyers and doctors. Close behind them are other highly educated specialists such as historians, economists, and scientists. Engineers fall in a slightly lower level but are still in the elite group. Below them come the majority who do not, properly speaking, have a profession. They are still differentiated, however, according to the classes of their work. Government officials rate highest; then come the military officers; and finally, down toward the bottom, are businessmen. The hierarchy does not stop there, however, because within the general sphere of business some fields have greater prestige than others. Banking, for example, is quite highly regarded, and accounting approaches the status of a respected profession. The man who is just a sales manager or a personnel manager or even a general manager has virtually no professional status, however.

The hierarchy in practice is often muddled because men's backgrounds may place them in two or more categories, e.g., the lawyer in government or the economist in business. However, the general stratification of society along professional lines is valid.

Except for the engineers and an occasional lawyer, the majority of the executives employed by United States companies are at the bottom of the scale. Their point of view and situation are summed up by Mr. Padilla, a controller. "Now, due to severe circumstances, some people will not go into a profession. They may be forced to leave school before they can complete their program. Those men have to go into work and they may start anywhere and make a career for themselves wherever they start. Or they may move from business to business as they have to. Their educational level is under that of the people who have completed their professional training. But it is still above the average, even if they do not have a degree. And then, too, they may actually be more successful than the people in the professions. They may make more money, particularly if they have good common sense and ability to manage business, but they don't have the professional label. That is important. It's a matter of pride and then, too, it's important in social affairs, in getting oneself in with the right people. If you're a lawyer or a doctor or an engineer, that helps you and you're in a better position to get money to work with."

Mr. Padilla expresses a variety of attitudes which are common in the Mexican culture. First, he establishes at the outset that business is an inferior occupation which a man accepts only when the doors to a profession are closed to him. Often, as with Mr. Padilla himself, the reason is economic. In many instances, however, the men who are forced into business are those who lack the character or intellect to meet professional standards. Mr. Padilla would not want to discuss that because it is a stigma which attaches to men in business and which able men like himself must fight constantly. According to the cultural standard, the best men go into the professions and those who do not, no matter how good their reasons, are always aware that they are considered professionally inferior.

Second, he expresses his own feeling about business as a career, which is not really a career at all but a situation which you make the best of. You start where you can, you shift around as you have to, and in time you may get ahead financially. There is no sense of pride evident here. He does not volunteer that he started in the lower ranks of the accounting field and has worked himself up to a senior position which is respected in the company, though this, in fact, is true and by United States standards Mr. Padilla has had a highly commendable career. If pressed to do so, he would build himself up along these lines. But speaking from his real feelings, he has no great pride in what he has done. It has been a makeshift existence which he has carried out as best he could. But all the while his mind has been on the career he did not have as a lawyer, the life which would have brought him real social respect and personal satisfaction.

Third, he places in perspective the value of money in contrast to professional status. Money is good and in a materialistic society it is a measure of success. Lack of money was the thing which deprived Mr. Padilla of his professional education. He knows it is worth a great deal. But he knows that it can never compensate for the lack of professional status.

Finally, as benefits an individualistic personality in an opportunistic society, he cites the practical value of the social position that the men of the professions hold. This element in Mexican life is related to the discussion of alliances in Chapter Two. We observed the utility of allies in the individualistic, competitive system. To perform effectively in business one must work through others: lawyers, engineers, bankers, and so forth. In view of the general cultural standards it is hard to find men one can trust beyond one's immediate family circle. The men with professional status fill part of this need. The long and quite expensive professional training period serves as a screening device so that the men who have professional status have an aura of respectability which invites the trust of others. There are, of course, unreliable men in the professions. But professional status at least distinguishes a man from the general run of business people, who are regarded as unscrupulous and unreliable. A Mexican will want to check up on any professional man he considers working with, but he will start with an assurance that the chances are good that he will be a better associate than the average businessman.

The characterization of the average businessman as unscrupulous and unreliable is in the main valid and it is the basis for the low prestige of the businessman in Mexico. Until recently business in Mexico has been dominated by trading and commerce. In Chapter Two the cultural codes of the trader were mentioned as one of the elements contributing to the development of the individualistic personality. The essence of the code is fierce competition with a minimum of concern for honesty, truth and reliability. Every man is on his own and the key to success is the ability to outwit and outmaneuver other traders. The men who achieve success in this struggle are admired for their skill, but their fellows can find no standard by which they deserve deep respect. To those immediately around them they are enemies. To broader society they are unconstructive parasites who milk the nation and its people for their own gain—the money lender with his high interest rates, the merchant with his exorbitant margins, and the sharp bookkeeper evading taxes.

To the trader there is nothing evil about his practices. They are all part of the game. He was reared to be a sharp trader and make money, and that is his way of life. But his activities create a problem for the professional manager who has a different role in society. We have already seen in Chapter Two that the individualistic attitudes which the trader society fosters are major impediments to the effectiveness of the executive in organizational relationships. Now we see the problem from another angle. In these societies, the word businessman is equated with the patterns of conduct of the trader. The distinction between the independent trader and the hired manager is not generally understood. The contributions of competition and private enterprise to general economic expansion, and the concept of professional management, with its teams of men devoted to increasing the efficiency of the movement of products through the production process and out into the hands of consumers, are foreign to their experience and can only be appreciated as they are demonstrated in practice. In the meantime, the professional manager, being part of "business," is associated with the image of "businessmen" as they have been known, which means the trader type of businessman.

Unfortunately, in the early stages of development of professional management in a country, the conduct of the hired manager often resembles that of the trader because hired managers find that they are more effective in dealing with the trader type of businessman if they adopt his methods. In the United States, where a very large portion of the economy is in the hands of hired managers, the development of a considerable level of mutual trust has been possible (though it is far from universal), and businessmen may be effective while still living by a high code of ethics. But where an executive deals day after day with men who are alert to trick him any way they can, there is a good chance he will learn to do things their way—an influence which applies even to United States executives.

This experience of Mr. Dunster, sales manager of the Thatcher Company, illustrates the problem. "I made a deal with Mr. Dominguez, our distributor in Guadalajara. We've been having trouble with the stores misrepresenting our products in their advertising. Dominguez has five dealers out there. I got him to promise not to make any more false claims. He even put it in writing, 'My organization will not represent the products of the Thatcher Company as performing in any way beyond the claims made in company specifications.' Now what happens? Two weeks ago I got reports that the dealers were at it again. I confirmed the reports and then complained to Dominguez. He said the dealers had a right to do just what they wanted. I showed him the letter and he said, 'I agreed that my organization would not misrepresent the products, but, you see, each of the dealers is an independent company and I can't force them to do things. You know people have their rights. I can't dictate to them from above.' Now I know perfectly well he owns every one of those dealers and they really snap when he wants them to, but I don't have a leg to stand on. You just have to be on your toes all the time with these fellows or they'll really take you."

Mr. Dunster, from all the evidence, was usually on his toes and he reported with a wry smile, "I go up to the home office and I tell them about these things and sometimes their eyes will open and you can see they're wondering just how much they can trust this Dunster fellow; whether he's not just as bad as these Mexicans he is talking about." The introduction of the word "bad" gives a typical United States cultural twist to this story. Mr. Dunster and Mr. Dominguez were not essentially concerned about whether they were good or bad in their dealings. They were doing business by a code which both understood and to a large degree enjoyed. However, their standards, along with those of countless other businessmen, both independent trader types and professional managers, did contribute to the public image of businessmen as people of low social value.

That is the basis for the low social status of business in Mexico and the same conditions generally apply in those large areas of Latin America, Africa, the Middle East and the Far East where industrialization is in its early stages and the standards of business conduct are set by the traders. In a perceptive analysis of Indian business society Helen Lamb describes the form these attitudes have taken in another culture:

> Business has the power of money, in India as elsewhere, but it does not have the prestige and general acceptance accorded business in the West. Some people attribute this to the widespread black marketeering and tax evasion by business during the wartime inflation and since. Recently India has produced some financial tycoons on the model of America's "robber barons," and they have not yet been transformed by public relations experts into industrial statesmen. But I think the low esteem in which Indian business is held is much more deep-seated. The goals and value system of business enterprise do not permeate Indian society as for instance they permeate our own. Indian business has had to operate in a cultural milieu which traditionally holds an organic view of society somewhat like that of feudal Europe. Individuals are members of a group to which they are subordinate, and relations between groups are harmonious and stable with each component performing its due function.[2] This view of society rules out liquidation of any group and reserves for Indian business, along with other elements, its due niche, but it is a subordinate one. Such an attitude is antithetic to those attributes of business enterprise which are equated with virtue in the West—competition, self-assertiveness, and the survival of the fittest, unremitting

[2] The difference between the group-subordinated and group-oriented societies is discussed in Appendix B.

innovation and the consequent revolution in methods of production and thereby in relationships among people—all set in motion by the profit motive. Modern Indian life has somewhat undermined the ancient view, always more of an ideal than a reality, but old conceptions linger on. The lofty disdain held by highly trained professional bureaucrats toward the humble money-lender origins of many of India's business families still persists and reflects the combined British-Indian cultural tradition in which government service constituted the greatest attraction. The conspicuous consumption of India's *merchant* princes seems to arouse more disapproval than that of her erstwhile titular princes among the many Indians to whom simplicity and austerity are valued for their own sake. Though there are notable exceptions, Indian business has not been very aggressive and venturesome in pioneering new industries for India. And this may be in part because the spirit of enterprise has not been glorified.[3]

In details the Indian situation differs from that in Mexico and the same is true elsewhere. The main features are similar, however. Business and businessmen are rated low on the scale because their practices and contributions are held in low esteem by society.

In Europe the status of the businessmen is different. There industrialization is far advanced and, as Harbison and Burgess observe, a managerial class is well established as distinguished from the petty bourgeois trading class.

Access to managerial positions is rigidly restricted. In the United States many people, including workers and union leaders, aspire to enter management, whereas in Europe only a select few ever have access to it. It is commonly understood in Europe that people get into management by virtue of being sons or heirs of existing owners, by marrying into the families of the owner dynasties, by using the leverage of a financial interest, or by acquiring a degree from a university or technical institution of higher learning. While this also happens in the United States, it is not so common a course as it is abroad. The European does not expect to work his way up into management from the ranks of the worker. . . .

In the United States, a qualified person can get into management without "a degree"; in Europe this is much more difficult. Yet in America about five times as many people (proportionate to

[3] Helen B. Lamb, "Business Organization and Leadership in India Today," published in a volume of papers prepared for The Seminar on Leadership and Political Institutions in India, University of California, Berkeley, August 12–17, 1956, pp. 10–12.

population) go to colleges and universities and get degrees than is the case in most European countries. Also, in the United States a very substantial proportion of persons in institutions of higher learning come from families with relatively little educational background, whereas the students in comparable institutions in Europe come predominantly from families already in the educated class. Thus in Europe business recruits its managerial personnel almost exclusively from the educated, whose numbers are already quite limited; in the United States business recruits its managers from the uneducated as well as from the educated even though the latter are proportionately much more numerous.

Thus the managerial group in France, Belgium, and Italy is a small and distinct elite. Since entry into the elite is restricted, management is decidedly class-conscious. Once admitted to the management class, either by education or through family connections, a person customarily acquires permanent tenure in the hierarchy.[4]

Thus there is pride and prestige in a management job, but there is still something different in the managerial status from that in the United States, where accomplishment in the business arena is respected for its productive value. These observations on the attitudes in the family managements which dominate much of French industry provide a key to European thinking:

> The business is not an end in itself, nor is its purpose to be found in any such independent ideal as production or service. It exists by and for the family, and the honor, reputation, and wealth of the one are the honor, wealth and reputation of the other.[5]

Implicit in these attitudes are the codes of social prestige found in most of the continent. Distinction is not based on economic productivity. It is based on honor, on breeding and on education. These attitudes are derived from earlier centuries when the men at the top of the social hierarchy were the nobility and the intellectuals they gathered around them. Positions in the managerial phases of business have been grafted onto this structure in the last century or so. They are essential to modern nobility and their codes of conduct have been set

[4] Frederick H. Harbison and Eugene W. Burgess, "Modern Management in Western Europe," *The American Journal of Sociology*, July, 1954, p. 17.
[5] David S. Landes, "French Business and the Businessman," *Modern France*, E. M. Earle, ed. (Princeton, N.J.: Princeton University Press), p. 336.

at a respectable level. Thus they have fitted in without disrupting the basic standards of the society. By contrast the boisterous, aggressive codes of United States industrial society are found relatively uncouth among the managerial elite of Europe.

But the acceptance of management men into the upper levels of European society does not mean that business accomplishment is itself the measure of a man's standing. To the contrary, it is the standards of the nobility and the literate which society counts as important and to which men aspire. Thus the businessman does not rate at the bottom of the hierarchy as he does in the trader societies, but he still has lower prestige than the members of the established professions and in many countries government service is considered a finer career than business.

The most important effect on business of its subordinate status in most of the world is that a management career does not generally attract the best men. On the whole there is little that the United States executive can do about that. By his actions he may contribute to the slow advance of the status of business, but in his immediate work it is a condition with which he can only learn to live.

Beyond this, the chief effect of the status of business noted in this research lay in the search for professional prestige among the foreign executives. Most Mexican executives are not, it appears, content to accept as final their existing professional status. Among the men I observed many were actively, and often successfully, working to better their position. Whereas economic status did not appear to most as a channel for significant progress because salary increases came slowly, advancement in professional prestige seemed feasible to them and worth considerable effort. For the most part the field of advancement lay outside the company organization, though they expected recognition of their achievements from their associates. The actual activities depended on the character of the man. A treasurer, for example, based his prestige on his standing in the banking world. He made the bankers club the center of his social activities and took great pride in his acceptance among important men in banking circles. Another man who evidently had hoped for a legal and government career, had developed excellent relations in government bureaus and took greatest pride in the fact that he was consulted from time to time on various government decisions.

Both of these men by the nature of their activities were, of course, helping the company. Their connections were very valuable in advancing their work. The quest of the foreign executive for status can often be an asset, therefore, and, judging by my observations, it is rarely an impediment to a man's work. Where it is a problem, it is usually because the United States executives do not recognize its importance to the foreign executives, and by their actions they hinder their associates in realizing their goals. This experience of Mr. Parsons, the production manager of the Reed Company, indicates the type of thing which can happen and the emotional effects it can have on a foreign executive.

Mr. Navarro, head of Reed's engineering department, was a member of a Mexican society of design engineers. He was younger than most of the group, but after a couple of years membership he was becoming known among them and felt that he was respected. The society was quite selective and, as no one in his department or elsewhere in the plant belonged, Mr. Navarro valued his membership highly. For one of the meetings the society decided to hold a "boss's" night and each member was to invite his superior to attend. Mr. Navarro was pleased that Mr. Parsons accepted his invitation and was looking forward to showing him off at the meeting because he was a more important man than the superiors of many of the other members. Then, the afternoon of the day of the meeting, Mr. Parsons got a wire from the home office demanding an immediate report on some excess costs in one of the sections of the plant. Mr. Parsons called Mr. Navarro in and told him he was very sorry but he would have to stay at the plant that evening and make up the report. He said, "I'm really sorry. I would have enjoyed going. But you go and have a good time."

Mr. Navarro didn't go. He called the secretary of the society and told him he was sick. Two years later this event was still deeply etched in his mind and he spoke with real bitterness about how Mr. Parsons did not appreciate the importance of professional design engineers. In fact, it did not appear from Mr. Navarro's character that design engineering meant much to him as such. He was a sensitive man to whom a sense of importance in any group was vital. He was inclined to build his position very carefully. In his own mind, his social status in Mexico had come to hinge largely on his importance in the society and he had thought of his triumphant presentation of Mr. Parsons to his associates as a master coup. Then with one quick stroke Mr. Parsons had destroyed the coup and placed the society at a level of importance below a mere report, and this for all the world—the people in the plant and the people in the society—to see and note. In short, Mr. Navarro was devastated.

Thus the low estate of business in the professional hierarchy is a factor which the United States executive must appreciate in understanding the state of mind of his foreign associates. This situation is not a static one, however, and a recent development in Mexico symbolizes a trend which is apparently starting in many societies. One of the side effects of the importance of professional status is the significance of titles in the Mexican culture. Each of the important groups in the Mexican professional hierarchy has a title which is used by men who have passed government qualifying examinations for their field. *Licenciado* (or Lic.), meaning technically, "licensed," is used by the lawyers and economists. *Doctor* applies to the medical men and to men in other fields who hold the top academic degree. A man with either of these titles is readily accorded respect. The engineers bear the title *Ingenierio* (or Ing.), and this distinguishes them from lesser groups, but its bearers are not introduced with the same pride. The military men, of course, have their own set of titles, but otherwise the groups below this educated elite had no titles until 1955. In that year, the government approved a university program or *carrera* in business administration (roughly equivalent to the master's or MBA program in the United States), thereby permitting its graduates to bear the title, *licenciado*. This development is a milestone in the evolution of Mexican society. The primary motivation of those who petitioned the government to approve the program was to project those who were highly educated in the science of management into the same social class as the economists. Most of the men behind the move were themselves *licenciados*, teachers of economics and law, who felt that the courses they were teaching gave men a caliber of intellectual training which justified the respect of society. Being oriented to the existing Mexican hierarchy, they saw the title as a necessary precondition for getting respect for their graduates.

The actual instigators of the movement were not consciously social revolutionaries, therefore. In fact, they were moderate conservatives in social matters. But the change they have achieved is revolutionary. It would not have been possible if the revolution had not already been underway and it will be some time before its effects are fully accomplished, but it is none the less a historic milestone. It means that henceforth a man may place himself close to the top of the prestige ladder through scholastic training in business. This recognition has been in the making for a number of years as the importance of the businessman to Mexican life has grown. Since World War II industrial expansion has held the spotlight in Mexico and the value of business-men to the country has been rated progressively higher. The govern-ment approval of the *carrera* was possible because of this general feeling and its own recognition of the need to encourage the develop-ment of good managerial personnel to accelerate the country's eco-nomic growth. As practical men they could see that more and better young men would chose administrative training if they could earn thereby the cherished *licenciado*.

Exactly how this change will work out cannot yet be determined. While the immediate justification is sound in relation to the economic and social evolution of the country, it is dubious in logical terms. Even in the United States, with its advanced interest in business training, administration is not classed as a profession in the same sense as medicine, law or learned fields like economics. In the true professions a reasonably well-defined body of knowledge is accepted as essential to effective work. The fields of activity are fairly well prescribed and proficiency in the practice of the profession can be predicted with some degree of success by the use of testing methods on the comple-tion of training. By contrast, the science of business administration is still in its adolescent, if not infant, years. The activities of the business-man cover a very wide and diffused field and the tests which measure a man's achievements in the training stage are generally conceded to be mediocre in predicting his competence as a practicing businessman.

Furthermore, only a few of the successful Mexican businessmen will probably ever hold the *licenciado* in administration. Despite the great growth of business schools in the United States, only a small portion of men in business, even in the younger generation, have received degrees in business administration. The *licenciados* in busi-ness administration are likely, therefore, to find themselves a small group with little actual status in the intellectual or business worlds. In some social circles the title will be helpful, but with many of their associates in business it may be more of an obstacle than a help. The young *licenciado* will usually find that men who have learned business by practicing it will expect him to prove his competence in action, and attempts to assert superiority by emphasis on the title will work to his disadvantage.

The ultimate effect of the change is more likely to be the fostering of the general rise in social prestige of businessmen through the dilution of the value of titles in general. Previously, the title *licenciado* was respected as designating men who were the skilled practitioners in their fields. It will lose some of its respect, however, if it simply signifies that a man graduated successfully from a course and is not necessarily among the successful practitioners of the skills he studied. If at the same time the untitled general run of businessmen continue their gradual rise in social status, we may expect something approaching the pattern in the United States, where titles have become relatively unimportant, membership in one of the professions giving a man some social status but not much more than that of the successful businessman.

The creation of the *licenciado* in administration appears in this light not as the birth of a new elite profession, but rather as part of the general upgrading of businessmen in the social hierarchy. As this process continues, its effect will be to make the hierarchy relatively less important and reduce the significance of professional status as a source of social prestige.

This sortie into the future is something of a digression from the attitudes which currently confront the United States executive abroad. It is useful, however, in illustrating the relative importance of professional status in foreign countries and the forces which may impede and encourage the evolution of the attitudes. Looking around the world we may sense that everywhere the importance of economic development is fostering the same type of evolution. In some places it is further advanced than in Mexico, while in others it is just beginning. The degree to which professional status is important to foreign executives will therefore vary from country to country. In general, however, it stands as a major element in their social motivations and one requiring the perceptive appreciation of the United States executive.

THE DYNAMICS OF MOTIVATION

"I've found that most of the executives abroad are not much concerned about getting into a new position. They concentrate on the job they're in and getting the most they can out of it. They work from day to day doing a good job to earn their daily bread. The idea of planning for future progression is much more a United States idea."

These observations of a widely traveled United States executive place in perspective the importance of the economic and social motivations of foreign executives. While numerous exceptions were observed in this research, the executive's generalization appeared to be well justified. The driving preoccupation with advancement which characterizes most executives in the United States is not common among many of their foreign counterparts. Their energies are directed at strengthening their present position and realizing the fullest satisfactions they can from it, with relatively little thought and effort devoted to achieving an upward step either in the organizational scale or in social life.

The Mexican situation does not appear in this respect to be representative, and the differences between it and other parts of the world are helpful in understanding the dynamic aspect of the motivations of executives. Among the Mexicans interviewed in this study was one who had worked with some six organizations, including at one stage a personally-owned company. Each change had represented to him a step forward, and with each company he had received one or more promotions, usually as a result of deliberate efforts on his own part. Another executive had throughout his working career set goals for advancement for the immediate future—usually five years. He had plotted out the progress in skills he would make for each stage and the promotions he would expect. His career had generally followed his plans, showing a steady upward progress, sometimes by promotions and twice by changing companies when promotion was blocked. There were also men who were obviously just drifting along in their work and not particularly anxious to get ahead. Because the research was concentrated on companies which were quite energetic in finding good local executives, the sample of men observed undoubtedly contained a greater portion of dynamic executives than would apply for all companies. None the less they were there, and there were ample indications that men of similar nature were scattered throughout industry.

In Europe and Asia the points of view are characteristically different. The typical European orientation is described by Harbison and Burgess:

> As one managing director said, "The goal of most of our executives is to make themselves as indispensable as possible. . . . Opportunities for younger executives are limited, incentives to assume responsibility are stifled, and taking initiative is not at-

tractive. . . . Once a member of management in a particular
company, a man is likely to remain there throughout his entire
career. It is unethical for one company to raid and woo executive
personnel from another. A person who leaves the company where
he has tenure as a member of management to accept a position
in another firm may be branded as a disloyal and unscrupulous
opportunist. For this reason vacancies are not likely to occur
frequently, and members of management jealously safeguard their
positions." [6]

Reports from Asian countries indicate the same general philosophy
—preoccupation with the protection of one's position and notably
less concern for progress.

The differences between foreign cultures in this respect parallel
the differences in attitudes toward innovation described in Chapter
Five and have much the same type of origins. In Mexico, life has been
generally unsettled for many decades. Opportunities for individual
progress have not been great but they have always been present, at
least for men with middle class backgrounds. The ambitious, capable
man has generally been able to find some avenue of advancement in
society. In earlier years the best opportunities lay in maneuvers through
and around the government hierarchy. More recently the economic
upsurge of the country has opened plentiful opportunities both for the
hired manager and the entrepreneur. In this environment a man may
entertain large ambitions with a reasonable chance of achieving them.
There are counter forces in the culture which limit the drive with
which men pursue their ambitions. As we saw in Chapter Three, the
Latin instincts do not run to the persisting, orderly effort which may
be needed to achieve objectives and, the class consciousness and
rigidities in Mexican society throw obstacles in the way of a man's
upward movement. But these elements are only deterrents and do not,
it appears from watching executives in action, prevent men from working hard for substantial goals and in many instances achieving them.

Other environments, however, are far less propitious for advancement, so the executive driving upward typically faces only frustration.
The basic aim of European business has been stability and security.
Supported by cartels, each company has clung to the status quo—a
given share of a market of fixed size. The economic boom which has

[6] *Op. cit.*, pp. 16–18.

swept through Europe in the 1950's is shaking this philosophy, but the cultural attitudes it fostered among the managerial class are well established. They visualize little opportunity to move ahead either within or outside their company, so they devote themselves to building as impregnable a position as possible for their existing jobs, giving little thought to advancement. Their motivations are applied dynamically in the sense that they pursue them energetically, but it is not a progressive dynamism.

In India and other countries a different type of problem leads to the same sort of attitude. As we saw earlier in the chapter, the slow pace of economic development does not provide enough opportunities to absorb the flow of educated men into the job market. A man must search diligently for a job. In many cases he obtains one only through the influence of relatives or friends and even then he may have to accept a position far below what he feels his capacities deserve. But knowing how scarce jobs are he is deeply grateful for what he has and, like the European, becomes primarily concerned with protecting his position. The chances of advancement are very small so it is a waste of time to devote his energies to that search.

All of this does not mean that men under these circumstances lose their desire for advancement. An experience in the Spencer Typewriter Company in India indicates the type of point of view which men may adopt. The company's operation had expanded from a sales office in the 1930's to a small assembly and sales unit in 1950. The organization had been built up steadily during this period by adding men as they were needed to do specific jobs, but without much in the way of systematic procedures. Except for the manager, the initial organization was composed of men who were effective in special tasks, such as selling and service, but were of relatively limited managerial capacity. Thus, as the scope of the operations grew, it had been necessary to bring in men of a higher caliber as executives.

In 1950, Mr. Mason, Spencer's vice president for foreign operations, decided some attention should be given to making the organization more orderly in a procedural sense. During a trip to India he suggested to Mr. Simpson, the personnel manager, that an organization manual be put together and efforts be made to hold the organization to it. Mr. Simpson devoted considerable time to the manual. He interviewed most of the people in the management and clerical staff, wrote up descriptions of their work and responsibilities, and established pay ranges for each position in consultation with Mr. Ross, the manager of the Indian unit. In 1951, Mr. Simpson left the company shortly after completing the manual.

While Mr. Mason was in India later in 1951, he had dinner with one of the senior accountants whom he had known for some time. In the course of the conversation Mr. Mason remarked that the men would probably miss Mr. Simpson, who, he knew, had been personally liked. The accountant said that he was missed and that he had been well liked. He observed, however, that in the last year there had been some talk against him because of "his program of freezing men in their jobs." On the whole, he felt that most people were not sorry to have him leave.

The accountant had not elaborated on this remark, but Mr. Mason, who had had long experience in India, felt he understood what he meant. The Indians on the staff had considerable ambition. Their ambitions might never be fulfilled and they probably realized this to some degree. However, as long as there was no specific ceiling set on their advancement, they were content in the thought that they might achieve substantial progress. The creation of the manual, with specific jobs and salary ranges, probably did not reduce the actual chances of advancement of any individual, but the men felt it had.

Looking broadly at the world, we see from these conditions that the dynamic quality in the motivations of executives differs greatly. In some cultures men are encouraged to believe that they can achieve substantial progress in their lives and many of them energetically pursue their objectives. In other cultures, upward progress is recognized as slow and difficult, so most executives throw their energies into protecting and making the most of their immediate position. Progress is hoped for and the dream of its realization is important for their satisfaction, but the pursuit of advancement does not loom large as an element in their regular activities.

SUMMARY

The range of motivational patterns which have appeared in this discussion underscores again the varied attitudes which the United States executive must be prepared to understand in his foreign associates. In summarizing the discussion, three basic guides for the executive in his search for understanding may be emphasized.

The first is the strong cultural influence in the formation of men's motivations. We have seen repeatedly that the character of the environment and the ideology are primary factors in establishing the objectives which a man feels are worthwhile. Both in the economic and the social aspects of life the standards of achievement which men set for themselves are frequently those which others in their society feel are desirable and laudable. And the character of the society, by establishing the opportunities for and obstacles to a man's progress, goes far in determining what objectives are realistic and thus worth seeking.

The second is the sense of the directions in which motivations may differ from expectations based on the United States cultural pattern. Seven main directions have been discussed: relations with other people, creativity, analysis, work discipline, economic gain, class distinction and professional status. These directions do not exhaust the types of motivational characteristics which United States executives will encounter, but they are the ones of greatest importance in the work of foreign executives. The ways in which men's attitudes run in each of these directions vary greatly from country to country and among individuals within countries, so each executive must be sized up as an individual. But an appreciation of the possibility of differences along the lines of these directions, with the probability that the differences will conform to the patterns induced by the culture, will help the United States executive in understanding each individual.

The third is an appreciation of the force with which the individual is in fact motivated toward his objectives—the dynamic aspect. Motivations may exist as anything from weakly felt desires to compelling drives. The expectations of United States executives are generally geared to the dynamic motivations of the modern managerial class in the United States. In some countries, like Mexico, motivations of comparable force are seen, but by and large, the tendency around the world is for a slower pace and less urgent drive for early realization of goals.

Chapter 5

Learning: Problems and Possibilities

To the dynamic United States executive, differing cultural traits in a foreign executive often appear as a missionary challenge. Convinced of the soundness of his own ways, he throws himself eagerly into the task of inducing the foreign executive to adopt the same approach to management. The executive is not a unique American citizen in this respect. As a nation our zeal to convert the world to our way of life seems to have no bounds, whether the subject is democracy, capitalism or baseball.

There is nothing wrong with this missionary zeal *per se*. Applied intelligently and sympathetically it can contribute significantly to the welfare of the world. In the area of the administrative attitudes of executives, however, the difficulties of accomplishment are such that a word of caution is in order as a starting point. Culturally-based attitudes do not change readily and the executive who expects rapid or substantial progress toward new attitudes is bound to be frustrated. It is well, therefore, to emphasize the values of understanding and adjustment on the part of the United States executive as more important to effective performance than skill in changing the ways of others. On the whole, the most productive executives abroad are those who thoroughly understand the types of differences we have seen in the last three chapters, and have found ways to run a business profitably within the bounds of management methods which are consistent with the attitudes of the foreign executives.

With this thought in the background, we can go on to consider the learning question—the problems which are involved in changing culturally-based attitudes and the ways in which change may come in an individual.

In the interests of clarity and brevity this chapter will deal solely with learning in the area of executive relationships, the problems discussed in Chapter Two. The essential aspects of the learning question are similar for all of the culturally-based attitudes which are discussed in this book. Some change more easily than others but the basic ways of approaching the learning process discussed below apply to all. From a presentation point of view it is easier to discuss the subject with reference to one set of attitudes, so that is the way the chapter is written.

The Blocks to Learning

To understand the problems involved in the learning process we must start with a picture of the impediments to learning. United States executives are frequently discouraged by the way foreign executives stick to their cultural attitudes when it appears that a change would obviously benefit everyone. To cite a typical case, there was the effort of Robert Rye to get Alphonso Rodriguez, one of his assistants, to speak more openly to his superiors. Shortly after Mr. Rye arrived in Mexico there was a substantial reorganization of the company in which a few management men were released. Mr. Rye thought that a real opportunity to change Mr. Rodriguez was at hand when the latter came to him and told him he felt insecure about his position and wondered what he could do to improve himself. Mr. Rye told him that he was considered technically superior in his field, but that the senior executives in the company felt that his failure to speak frankly was a real shortcoming. He made quite a speech to Mr. Rodriguez about the need for upward communication and, when Mr. Rodriguez showed interest and promised to improve, he felt quite elated. As the months progressed, however, nothing happened and it became clear that Mr. Rodriguez either could not or would not develop into a satisfactory executive in this respect.

Why should a change like this be so hard for Alphonso Rodriguez? The answer to that question lies in a composite of forces which make for stability of personalities in any society. These are the influences from within and without the individual which hold him to a more or less consistent course in life. They have real value in maintaining the effectiveness of the society and of the individuals within it. But in the process they also serve as blocks to learning. This composite of forces is not readily disentangled, but three elements in it may be singled out as playing a major role: habit, cultural reinforcement, and learning attitudes.

Habit

While the strength of habit may be obvious, it is worth belaboring it a little to assure full appreciation of its power over a man. The fact that certain attitudes and methods of conducting relationships are part of a culture means that the individual has grown up regarding them as natural. They compose a pattern of behavior which people have expected of him since he was a child, and he has found that he could get by in society if he lived by their dictates. All of this is largely at the subconscious level, since a man's pattern of behavior is only to a limited extent the result of day-to-day deliberate decisions.

For Alphonso Rodriguez, not speaking up to superiors was a deeply-rooted personality trait. Throughout his childhood it was quite clear to him that he had no business expressing his own opinions to his father, or his teachers, or the priest. On the few occasions when he had done so, it had been made painfully clear to him that he had done the wrong thing. He and his friends whose experiences were similar had adjusted to this condition quite readily. He could feel comfortable in the presence of superiors, accepting their authority and forgetting his own views so long as he was with them. To change all that would require deliberate action. He would not know exactly how one played such a role, and in attempting to play it he would feel ill at ease. Such is the power of habit.

Cultural Reinforcement

The same forces which create habits tend to propagate them. Mr. Rye may enter into Mr. Rodriguez' life, exerting an influence in a new direction, but most of his relationships continue to be with his own culture. His family, his friends, the men he does business with, the people he reads about in newspapers and novels, and the many other elements in his life influenced him to be what he is, and they will support him in continuing as he is. Even within the company most of his associates will be Mexicans whose attitudes are more likely to be like his own than Mr. Rye's.

Under these circumstances acceptance of Mr. Rye's suggestion requires that Mr. Rodriguez assume one of two possible positions with relation to other parts of his society. He must either break with the pattern of his culture or learn to live by both cultures. Either position is possible, but they are both difficult.

The man who gives up his native culture is likely to lose effectiveness both in his social contacts and in the business world, a problem which was discussed in Chapter Two. For example, if Mr. Rodriguez learns to speak frankly with superiors and carries that practice over into his relations with government officials he is likely to be labeled, along with many United States executives, as crude and insolent, except that, unlike the United States executives, he will not be pardoned as an ignorant foreigner.

The other possibility, the bi-cultural position, is both feasible and effective. However, as any United States executive who has worked abroad knows, it is difficult. Except in the advanced stages of accomplishment, one must be constantly thinking about the character of situations, figuring out what attitudes are appropriate and acting with deliberation—a tiring and uncomfortable existence by comparison with conformance to habit.

Mr. Rodriguez would not explicitly think out the alternatives in this way, but his environment, in a sense, puts it to him that way. "Here," it says, "you've come a long way living by our rules. Maybe you are a little worried about your job right now, but look how far you've gone and how many people among your countrymen respect you as you are. We are not asking you to change, and if you do, you have no way of knowing how well you will get along with us." So men often don't change, perhaps losing out a little in their position in the eyes of United States executives, but comfortable and effective in their own society.

Learning Attitude

One of the striking features of the field research for this study was the almost complete lack of interest on the part of the Mexican executives in learning at the level we are considering here (i.e., administrative attitudes as distinguished from techniques). Only two, both of them young men who had had rather exceptional educational experiences, including extended stays in the United States, spoke intelligently about changes in their own attitudes. The rest were essentially lacking in what I shall call a learning attitude. Some of them talked a good deal about learning to be better executives but always in terms of mechanical types of adjustments, not changes in their own attitudes. When they talked about delegation, for example, they mentioned physical transfers of work and even of responsibility, but not detaching themselves emotionally from the delegated work or changing from a directing to a guiding relationship with the subordinate.

At the root of this situation is a state of mind common to relatively stable cultures which can be better understood if we look at an extreme case. Elton Mayo describes the position of the individual in a society of rigid cultural attitudes:

> In these primitive communities there is room for an individual to develop skill, but there is no latitude for the development of radical or intelligent opinions. If he develops special prowess in hunting or war he gains mana and reputation; but he is not expected to develop any intelligent thinking about details of social organization. The unit is, in a sense, the group or commune, and not the separate individuals;[1] the development of anything in the nature of personal capacity must be subordinate to the whole. With us it is quite otherwise; the intent of education in a complex society is to develop intelligence and independence of judgment in the individual. The primitive community develops social intelligence and not individual intelligences. Over almost the entire area of a man's life society thinks for him; and he learns only the social responses he must produce in reply to given signals. This is a very restricted method of living, but it is highly integrate and "functional"; in addition to this it is very comfortable for the individual, who does not need to wrestle with a solitary problem.[2]

The Mexican culture has, of course, never been so rigid or simple as that of the primitive tribe and today the areas of change are great. None the less, in the significant attitudes which we have discussed, the forces for cultural uniformity are strong and the essential psychology described by Mayo is present.

---

[1] Again reference is made to the discussion of individualism and group submission in Appendix B.
[2] Elton Mayo, *The Human Problems of an Industrial Civilization* (Boston: Division of Research, Harvard Business School), 1946, pp. 149–150.

For example, the average Mexican of the generation who are now executives grew up with a clear sense that superior-subordinate relations were established along the authoritarian lines described in Chapter Two. This pattern provided him with some options (e.g., full submission or evasive submission) but otherwise the character of the relationship was not something he thought about. It was part of life and he lived it. As new phases of life came along like assuming the position of a superior, he readily absorbed them by imitation and experience.

These executives have learned, but the ability to learn is different from the learning attitude, and the distinction is significant to our problem. While the characters of these men have gone through some changes they have not really been conscious of it and they have not noticed it in others. Therefore, the idea of personality change is not part of their thinking. It is not that they do not want to change but rather that the possibilities and mechanisms for change are unknown.

Given this point of view, a man's attitudes may change, if conditions in his environment force him to; but he has little capacity to initiate a deliberate effort for change within himself. Alphonso Rodriguez did not, in fact, want to conform to Mr. Rye's suggestion, but if he had, he probably would not have known where to start. He had never in his life sat down with a question like, "Maybe when I'm with superiors, I feel too submissive. I think I'll try to get hold of myself once in a while and argue my point of view with them." The ability to do such a thing requires a learning attitude which is not common even in the supposedly fluid United States culture. In most foreign cultures it is notably lacking and the possibilities of learning are accordingly lessened.

THE POSSIBILITIES OF LEARNING

The combined effects of habit, cultural reinforcement and lack of learning attitude limit sharply the possibilities of changing the attitudes of an individual. But there is also a hopeful side to the picture which can be seen both in the general change in cultures and in the progress of specific individuals.

A great many of the cultures of the world appear to be changing and within these cultures the possibilities for developing new attitudes in individuals are greater than in static cultures. Furthermore, the process of cultural change seems particularly favorable to development of the types of administrative attitudes which are effective for industrial management.

In virtually all countries industrialization is advancing rapidly or the structure of existing industries is changing, forcing modifications in old ways of life and established cultures. So far as administrative relationships are concerned there is further encouragement to change in the evolution of new patterns of conduct in the family and other institutions. One observes, for example, a slow but still very sure shift toward more democratic parental relations.

The modification of cultures proceeds in a halting and irregular manner. Among some groups or in certain localities progress is much faster than in others. There is no guarantee, therefore, that all executives will be encouraged in their personal development. In fact, from my observations the intelligent, energetic young men who become executives are typically the more advanced members of their societies in the development of new attitudes, so they are as likely as not to be impeded by their countrymen. But the general trend is still there, assuring possibilities of finding people who are breaking ahead of the pack, and a fluid enough culture so that they will not be inhibited at every turn by static attitudes.

These general conclusions are confirmed by evidence of change in specific individuals. Several executives were observed in this study who had moved appreciably away from earlier attitudes which were more typical of the Mexican culture. On a broader scale, a number of recent studies indicate that foreign students in the United States frequently adopt new attitudes and that at least a part of this learning is retained when they return home.[3] The learning conditions for these groups are different from the on-the-job development experiences of the typical executive. Most of the students are young people who have enough interest in the ways of others to venture abroad, and they spend quite extended periods away from the influence of their home cultures. For our purposes, however, their experiences are interesting in that they confirm the possibilities of change in an individual and the basic characteristics of the learning process as they appeared in the smaller sampling of people covered by the current

[3] Ralph L. Beals and Norman D. Humphrey, *op. cit.;* John Useem and Ruth Hill Useem, *op. cit.;* Jeanne Watson and Ronald Lippitt, *op. cit.*

research. The fundamental aspects of accomplishing changes in attitudes seem to be common to all conditions.

In analyzing the learning processes of executives, two distinctions as to levels of accomplishment appeared helpful in this study. The first is the distinction between changes in formal behavior and changes in personality and attitudes. The second is that between attitudes applied to personal actions and attitudes applied to expectations of others. These distinctions will be spelled out at length because they were observed to be important both in the character of the change which each required, and in the implications they held for management effectiveness.

Formal Behavior

There are a great many executives who have accepted the desirability of new patterns of administrative action and who incorporate part of these patterns into their own work, but whose natural attitudes continue to run counter to them. This is the formal behavior level of learning. Many people do not classify it as learning at all, preferring to reserve that term for alterations in basic attitudes. Regardless of the term we use, however, it does represent a change from the action pattern of the man who both feels and acts according to his initial attitudes. It is significant because of its effect on an executive's performance and because the United States executive observing it is likely to be confused as to its meaning.

Mr. Tela was typical of the men at this level of learning. Mr. Tela had all of the characteristics of the individualistic personality. He was ambitious and had read a wide range of books and articles on the subject of management. It was quite clear to him that communication vertically and horizontally made an organization more effective, that delegation of responsibility would increase output down the line, and that cooperating with others was helpful in getting jobs done. He could talk very lucidly and forcefully about these concepts of management. In much of his daily work he conformed to what he understood to be their requirements. He spent much of his time on the phone or visiting around the office taking up matters with other executives. He specifically delegated certain functions to subordinates and he put considerable effort into instructing them to follow similar practices. None of this came naturally to him, however. Each action was consciously planned and deliberately carried out as part of his program to make his section productive and to make himself more valuable in the eyes of the senior executives in the company. He was quite sincere in believing that what he was doing was good for the company, but this belief had had little effect on his own attitudes.

The prevalence of men like Mr. Tela in Mexico is related to the attitudes toward change and United States industrial success discussed in Chapter Three. Most ambitious Mexican executives have a profound respect for United States management methods. They read a great deal about them and attempt to apply them to their work. But many do so without much discrimination or thought. Advertising ideas and delegation techniques are absorbed and applied with equal ease, both being looked on as functional parts of the machine of a modern industrial organization. Rarely is thought given to the possibility that something like delegation may involve fundamental personality changes if it is to be effective. Norman Humphrey observes that this blindness is found throughout Mexican society, the people having adopted a variety of the superficial aspects of United States life without realizing their impact on Mexican culture. For example, "Few have thought through the 'undesirable' effects such things as the introduction of 'desirable' trucks and automobiles will have on seemingly unrelated areas of strong emotional-cultural value which they want to retain, like the continued protection and seclusion of women." [4]

The adoption of the practices of the group-oriented type of personality on the formal behavior level can contribute appreciably to an executive's effectiveness. A large portion of the time, Mr. Tela's actions resembled those of a man who really felt like communicating, cooperating, and delegating. He was awkward about it sometimes but he did it, and other people were more effective because they received information from him, got his help on jobs, and were given opportunities to make their own contributions.

But there are limits to how far such a man can go. Under strain or

[4] Norman D. Humphrey, "The Mexican Image of Americans," *The Annals* (Philadelphia: The American Academy of Political and Social Science), September, 1954, p. 119.

in special situations he will usually revert to the individualistic pattern of action. This results in reduced effectiveness in the immediate situation and it sets limits on the beneficial attitudes which he can build up around him. For example, Mr. Tela was assigned to work as chairman of a group developing plans for the introduction of a new product. The group included men from production, advertising and finance, each of whom made major contributions to the project. When their work was done Mr. Tela drew up the report and presented it to the manager with his own name appearing prominently at the top as author and only a minor note buried in the report about the work of the others. As a result of this and similar incidents, the willingness of others to cooperate with Mr. Tela never advanced far and they often went out of their way to play up his shortcomings to his boss.

For the United States executive the man who has achieved considerable skill at the formal behavior level may present a major problem. Since a prime objective of adopting the new methods is to appear in a favorable light to the boss, the executive will usually make a major effort to follow the "right" practice when the boss is around. He will talk about such things as cooperation, he will go through the approved motions in committees, and so on. During the research for this study I was fascinated by the adroitness of men at this art and at the success they had in convincing their superiors. This, of course, is part and parcel of the skill of the individualistic personality in dealing with the boss.

The problem for the United States executive lies in the possibility of making errors in management decisions because he has been fooled. For example, Mr. Thorp, the general manager of the Zwicker Company, was concerned over the inadequacy of production of some products. He talked to Mr. Reyes, the production manager about it. Mr. Reyes said that the problem lay in the inability of the purchasing agent, Mr. Prado, to understand fully the problems of procuring supplies for these products but he suggested that Mr. Thorp not talk to Mr. Prado. He said that he had been working with Mr. Prado for some time on the matter and he felt that Mr. Prado was beginning to learn what was needed. Mr. Thorp had noticed in meetings and other aspects of his work that Mr. Reyes showed a good grasp of the problems of other departments and seemed sympathetic with their point of view, so he accepted Mr. Reyes' opinion and did no more about the matter. In fact, however, the basic problem lay in Mr.

Reyes' own department. He made no effort to make certain that the purchasing department knew of requirements in time to assure deliveries. Mr. Prado was not pleased with this situation, but so long as no one complained he was content to avoid a dispute with Mr. Reyes, who he knew was a smarter talker than he.

Personality Change—Personal Conduct Level

Learning at the level of personality is quite a different story from changes in formal behavior. It involves a real change in the attitudes of a man. Observable changes in conduct are not deliberate deviations from instinctive actions. Rather, they are valid manifestations of a new outlook on life. The change in the attitude toward subordinates of Mr. Jimenez described in Chapter Two (page 37) is a good example. He had not just learned about training and delegating as mechanical skills. The idea of helping to develop the capacities of people had caught his imagination and he had become emotionally committed to that philosophy. Once that type of change has come in a man, the pattern of action of the group-oriented personality becomes instinctive with him. Comparing him with the man at the formal behavior level, we may judge his actions to be a true reflection of his feelings, and therefore expect that they will be consistent even under stress or unusual conditions.

For the United States executive there is a world of difference between working with a man who is at the formal behavior level and one who is at the personality change level. Whereas he must be constantly alert with the former to discern the true meaning of his actions, he can take the latter's actions at face value. This, of course, is something of an oversimplification because there are many men who may fall in one level in some respects and the other in some. However, the degree of alertness required of the United States executive goes down as the degree of personality-level learning by the foreign executive increases and, as we observed in Chapter Two, there are many foreign executives whose basic attitudes are essentially those required for high organizational effectiveness.

Personality Change—Expectation Level

At the expectation level the change in personal attitudes affects the standards which the individual sets for the performance of others.

Such learning is complex in nature and the findings in this research were insufficient to justify discussing it at length. However, a few significant aspects of the subject were apparent from my observations and are worth reporting in view of their importance for management policies.

It seems to be quite uncommon for a man's expectations of others to change greatly from the standards common to the national culture. Though his own attitudes may have changed considerably, an executive does not necessarily expect similar changes in those around him.

The reasons for this dual standard are not hard to find. While the individual may change it is unlikely that those about him, particularly those outside the company, will change with him. To expect them to change would result in frustration, disfavor by others, and a loss of effectiveness. Most foreign executives will therefore continue to judge the actions of others by the standards of the culture. For example, Mr. Lozano had, in the course of time, acquired quite completely the attitudes of the group-oriented personality and he was very effective in cooperating with other executives. He could argue with them when occasion arose and still maintain their respect and trust. He knew, however, that this capacity was not common among his countrymen and he did not expect it of his subordinates. Instead, he took pains to see that when any troublesome issues with other departments arose, his men should bring them to him and let him work them out. In this manner, he assured that the subordinates would have reasonably good relations with other departments even though their personalities did not change.

The extent of an executive's learning at the expectation level is significant in his capacity to advance the learning of others. In the next section we shall consider the influence of the superior in the learning process. Suffice it at this point to observe that it is important. The superior cannot by his expectations enforce change in a subordinate, but if he does not have any expectation of change or encourage learning, then learning will be retarded. This observation applies to all levels of foreign executives. It has special significance, however, if the executive is the senior man in a foreign unit. The policy of placing local nationals in management positions now has wide acceptance among United States concerns and most of them are moving rapidly in replacing United States executives with local men.

But turning over the top job to a national remains a troublesome question. Many enlightened and intelligent United States managements frankly express unwillingness to take that step and the experience of others confirms their doubts. While there are several factors involved in their thinking, this question of the degree of change in the expectations of the executive appears a crucial consideration. They observe that an executive may himself demonstrate all of the qualities they regard as essential (the personal conduct level) and under the leadership of a United States executive he may even have developed and enforced such qualities in subordinates, but they doubt if he would maintain these standards against the counter-pressures of the national ideology when the leadership is removed. To support their position they cite specific cases in which foreign executives who had seemed highly competent proved unable to hold an organization up to the standards the United States management had set. In this research I did not actually observe any cases of this sort. In fact, the only senior Mexican I observed in action seemed to be doing an exceptional job in these respects and his home office was more than satisfied. Nonetheless, my observations of the level of change in the standards of men in the second and third tiers of management did indicate that few men would meet this severe test.

How Men Learn

This three-level system of classification is useful in describing the ways in which men change and sets the stage for the next question— how they change. What forces encourage them to learn what they learn and what prevents their learning more? For each executive there are distinctly personal and fairly complex answers to these questions. We cannot hope to understand all of the forces present in each case, but we can observe some, especially those external factors in which the United States executive plays an important role.

Since learning is such an individualized process, it is well to commence its analysis with the learning histories of three individuals. It should be noted that these histories are based on the recollections of the men and observations of their current situations. They are not complete, therefore, but they tell enough to indicate the types of learning forces at work.

Raul Ortega was from an early age ambitious and independent. He came from a good family but had preferred to make his own way in the world. He was always restless and anxious to advance himself, and he took considerable satisfaction in improving the effectiveness of the business operations at which he worked.

He had served with several companies in his career. As soon as he moved to a new position he started planning a process of advancement. He would establish his own competence in the work and find ways to demonstrate to men in higher management that he was superior to his immediate boss or someone else in the next echelon. He would then be advanced to the higher position, from whence he would start his maneuvers for the next move up.

Mr. Ortega had progressed in his early years largely because of his technical competence coupled with thoroughness and hard work. As he moved up the ladder, however, he observed that management skills were expected. His superiors talked a good deal about such requisites of good executives as leadership, delegation, and cooperation. Mr. Ortega, therefore, studied up on these skills and developed a capacity to apply them in much of his work. Combining these with the vast knowledge of his field of business acquired as he worked up through the ranks, a mixture of hard boiled and shrewd techniques in supervising his men, and hard work on his own part, he maintained a quite effective operation beneath him. His immediate superior in his latest job was impressed both with his results and his apparent competence in executive skills. His superior was a good deal like Mr. Ortega. He was intellectually interested in promoting such things as cooperation among his subordinates, but his own instincts were of the authoritarian-individualistic type and they showed up in many ways in his daily work. Mr. Ortega's associates had varied opinions about his cooperativeness, but they had no occasion to express them and in the interests of their own advancement they found it advisable to cooperate with him.

Miguel Fernandez was also ambitious and independent. At an early stage in his career his point of view toward his relations with others was shaken. He felt the turning point came after a year in a graduate school in the United States for which he had won a scholarship on the basis of his brilliance. "When I was in college, I heard about the chance of that scholarship and I went all out to win it. All I was doing was working for myself. That's all I ever thought about. When I came back, I realized that that wasn't the thing. That wasn't what was going to get me ahead. It wasn't going to help me to be arguing all the time and fighting with other people." In fact, the trip probably was just a part of a general learning process which went on for a long period. "That's something you learn out of the environment you're in. You learn by watching people and seeing who gets ahead. You can see that some people are getting ahead and some people aren't, and you can figure out pretty fast that the ones who are getting ahead are the ones who are learning how to manage people and run an organization."

As his career advanced Mr. Fernandez found himself in varied positions. His vivid memories were all in terms of the problems these jobs had posed in the application of his ideas about working with people. He recalled with particular vigor a few major successes, including a case where he had come into an organization broken up into isolated and jealous groups and had by skillful leadership brought them together as an effective working team.

His current job posed something of a problem for Mr. Fernandez. It paid well and provided broader work experience than any he had had before. His superior, however, was something of a prima donna. He was inclined to keep a large amount of control in his own hands, to by-pass subordinates, and to grab credit away from others in the organization. Mr. Fernandez' abilities were so widely recognized that his superior had no choice but to give him credit when it was due. Mr. Fernandez had been able to develop relationships which he regarded as quite satisfactory with men immediately around him. From time to time, however, he was disappointed because others in the organization did not meet him half way. With these people he had developed a pattern of relatively "hardboiled," legalistic relationships which assured satisfactory accomplishment of essential functions, but not much in the way of constructive cooperative effort. To the observer it appeared that the current situation was unstable and that before long one of three things must happen to Mr. Fernandez: (1) that under the pressures of the general organizational situation he would revert to the character he had when his career started, (2) that he would replace his superior, or (3) that he would leave to find a more congenial atmosphere.

Pedro Carvajal, like the others, was ambitious and independent. His first job was as maintenance engineer with the Rollins Company. His first significant project was reorganizing the company's toolroom, which was a mess at the time. His description of the project tells a good deal about his character:

Carvajal: "I got two boys to help me. I set up a system of classes of tools and then we worked at sorting the mess out and setting up a usable toolroom. We worked really hard. I told the boys that was the way it had to be. We worked seven days a week. We worked on Saturdays and Sundays. It got kind of tough, too. It was a dusty job, and I got a little grippe, I think. But I kept on coming in and working. At the end of the month we had it done. I called up Mr. Fish [the production manager] and said, 'You can come around and take a look. You've got a toolroom now.' He came around and said, 'You've done a really good job.' I told him that the credit shouldn't go to me. The credit belonged to the boys who had done the bulk of the work."

Observer: "Why did you say that? Actually, you had done a large part of the work and it was your responsibility, wasn't it?"

Carvajal: "That's true, but I didn't want to get credit for myself. You see, I'd been really whipping those boys. I'd been pushing them hard. I think probably they hated me by the time we got through with the work. I think they thought I was doing it all for myself, that I was going to grab all the credit and I was going to get all the benefit for the work, in the eyes of Mr. Fish."

Observer: "There was some truth in that though, wasn't there? You really did want to get credit for doing the job."

Carvajal: "Yes, I did. I wanted to get ahead, but I didn't want Mr. Fish to see it that way. I knew he wouldn't like it if he thought I was trying to grab all the credit away from the boys."

Mr. Fish had taken over the production department not long before that and in time did a major job of getting it to functioning well. He eliminated a number of men he felt were incompetent. While this created some animosity, he was, on the whole, respected as being absolutely fair in his judgments. He kept only men in whom he had confidence. He gave them wide freedom of action and he was helpful to them when they came to him with problems. Mr. Carvajal was very happy working with Mr. Fish and the group he had gathered around him.

Mr. Carvajal's learning process is hard to describe because he was never conscious of it and it was rather diffuse. Comparing his current actions with the toolroom story and other early incidents it was clear that he had changed. The chief change was that the premeditated self-advancement character of his cooperative actions had largely disappeared. Judging by similar current incidents, if the toolroom experience were repeated today, his reply to Mr. Fish's praise would be something like, "Thanks, we think we did a good job." He would say it without thinking and it would be accepted without much reaction by anyone. The boys would have full confidence that he really did appreciate their work and that quite probably he would say something more to Mr. Fish about their efforts after they had left. Mr. Fish would take it for granted that Mr. Carvajal accepted praise for himself and his subordinates as inseparably related, since he had picked and trained them and their good work was what was helping him to get ahead. But no well-planned set of words would be necessary to convey these ideas. They would be understood without anything being said, so the exchange between Mr. Fish and Mr. Carvajal would be just a formality.

Mr. Carvajal still devoted a lot of time to premeditated planning in his relationships with people, but it was of a different nature. For example, having advanced to the position of production manager, he had become much concerned that people in sales should understand production problems and vice versa, so that product design, scheduling, and so forth should be more effective. His first target had been the sales manager. His plan was to intrigue and involve the sales manager by gradually making more and more production problems joint problems. The fact that the two men had already known each other for some time and had had a variety of contacts which had been satisfactory, helped. At the end of two years he reported that his plan had borne fruit. "Now, he's beginning to see the production side of things a great deal more. I find it much easier to talk with him as he's beginning to get the production viewpoint very well." Thus encouraged he had launched into the broader objective of getting the junior sales executives and the sales force production-oriented.

An accumulation of everyday experience seemed to add up to this change in Mr. Carvajal. As we gather from the toolroom story he was sensitive to the feelings of people from the start. As time went on he found repeatedly that it was rewarding both in Mr. Fish's praise and in getting jobs done to recognize these feelings and to do what he could to accommodate them. People's confidence in him grew and he came to be regarded as a helpful person. A host of little incidents make up the picture. For example, when Mr. Ramos, who had been in production, was made service manager, Mr. Vilchis, the assistant service manager, found Mr. Ramos' actions hard to understand. So it was natural that he came to Mr. Carvajal, and the latter, talking to him a little and to Ramos a little, helped them to work out the problem.

In each of these cases, change has taken place in the men. Some of it appears as the result of a conscious, deliberate effort; some as an unconscious process of assimilation; much of it both conscious and unconscious. The conscious changes seem more important because they are explicit in the minds of the men and are more readily recorded in the brief stories. But they are not necessarily the commonest or most significant forms of learning. In fact, over the course of a man's life the greater portion of his learning is probably of the assimilative type. Certainly the learning of children is very largely of that character and throughout life men acquire much of their behavioral patterns and attitudes from unconscious imitation and conditioning.

Among the men observed in this research a large portion of the conscious change seemed to result in progress only to the formal behavior level. That is, Mexican executives were quite astute in grasping the patterns of behavior which were desired by their superiors and modifying their actions accordingly. However, lacking a real learning attitude, most of them were unable to proceed consciously to a higher level. They did not perceive that changes in values and attitudes were either possible or valuable. Only a minority had enough insight and objectivity in seeing themselves to consider questioning and modifying their basic personalities. Thus, while it is commendable for the United States executive to encourage deliberate efforts at self-improvement among his associates, the expectations of these efforts must not be too great. Fairly rapid and effective changes at the formal behavior level may be forthcoming. But changes in personality are more likely to come as a result of a slow process of unconscious adjustment.

For the individual these two types of learning processes are quite different. The conscious method involves an intellectual determination of the desirability of accomplishing a change, and the deliberate effort to adjust to its requirements. The unconscious method is by definition an unplanned and scarcely observed progression. The exact way in which change may come in foreign executives does not, however, appear as a matter which need greatly concern the United States executive because very similar actions on his part seem to foster both types of learning. Whether or not learning will take place and the way in which it proceeds depend very largely on the individual foreign executives and a host of other elements in their lives. The United States executive is at best a marginal influence. He can do little to affect the way in which foreign executives go about their personal development. What influence he has lies chiefly in two aspects of the learning process: (1) the initiation of the desire for change and (2) the testing of new approaches in experience. In singling out these two aspects as a focus for analysis, I am grossly oversimplifying the erratic complex of perceptions, experiences, and conflicts which make up the learning process. It is of practical value, however, as a means of pointing out the effect which the actions of the United States executive may have.

The Initiative for Change

The learning process must start at some point. In conscious learning that point may be quite well defined, e.g., an idea gleaned from reading a book, or a new approach conceived in reflecting on a failure. In unconscious learning, defining the inception of the process is much harder, but it is there nonetheless. In both cases, it is possible for the initiative for change to be purely internal but this seems to be rare. Some external force or condition is part of the initiative for most changes. Mr. Ortega's ideas came from listening to superiors and reading books, Mr. Fernandez observed the ways of other executives, and the changes in Mr. Carvajal were inspired by Mr. Fish. The first two were generally conscious processes while the latter seemed only partly so and partly a gradual unconscious imitation and reaction process. Regardless of the process, however, the changes in each man were started, at least in part, because of an external influence.

New ideas may enter into the minds of executives in a variety of ways. As most men who reach the management level are ambitious, a disposition to look for new ideas which will help them is usually present. They are willing to entertain intellectually any likely idea they come across. In the give and take of daily business they have some degree of sensitivity at the reaction level to different patterns of action which they may absorb and imitate. The circumstances appear favorable, therefore, for the United States executive to contribute readily to this phase of the learning process. However, there is one significant element in the relations between United States and foreign executives which frequently impedes his efforts. That is the sensitivity of the foreign executives. The causes of this sensitivity will be discussed at length in the next chapter. Suffice it at this point to observe that most foreign executives are very sensitive to criticism (as are a large portion of United States executives). The possibilities of starting a man on the road to learning by direct suggestion of change are therefore limited.

During this study a variety of effects were observed from direct efforts by United States executives to initiate change in subordinates. In a few cases the subordinate had left the company. Rather than taking the suggestion as an effort by the superior to help him to do a better job, he understood it to mean that he was not appreciated. These cases might be discounted as representing undesirable men who were probably not worth having anyway, except that a number of competent United States executives felt their point of view was representative and that they would rarely criticize a man directly because such a reaction was always possible.

A more common reaction to criticism was silent acquiescence and rejection. The case of Alphonso Rodriguez described at the beginning of this chapter is typical. Mr. Rodriguez did not really understand what Mr. Rye was proposing. What he did understand was that Mr. Rye was challenging what he was. His reaction was consistent with the character of the individualistic personality. He withdrew within himself, protecting himself from the challenge, and not only did not accept the new idea but set up emotional barriers against it.

With enough persistence the direct approach can, of course, get an idea solidly into the mind of the individual, though with unfortunate effects on working relationships. Situations in this category vary but one story will illustrate their nature. John Miles told the author that he was working hard to get Mr. Salas to cooperate more with other department heads. He had told Mr. Salas specifically that this was a shortcoming and he kept after him by questioning him frequently about the extent of his cooperation on specific problems as they came along, pointing out ways in which he could have done more. Mr. Salas had built his whole career around that company, so leaving would have been an extreme solution and some type of action was obviously necessary to placate Mr. Miles. So he had absorbed the idea of what Mr. Miles wanted and went through the motions of cooperative effort to a considerable degree. In talking with the author, however, he virtually ignored the existence of Mr. Miles. He made some references to a former superior and to a man in the home office, both of whom he evidently liked, and he was not averse to giving them credit for help in his own work. But he apparently regarded Mr. Miles as an unpleasant element in his life and certainly not a person who was helping him to do a better job. It is not impossible that Mr. Miles had started a learning process which ultimately would be beneficial, but for the time being his efforts had impaired his own relationship with a subordinate so that cooperative effort between them was at a low level.

The type of relationship which Mr. Miles had established has potential effects on the learning process in another way. It decreases the satisfactions which the subordinate finds in his work and this will probably increase the importance to him of satisfactions he may find elsewhere, for example in his home, or with business associates outside the company. The strength of cultural reinforcement of attitudes as a block to his learning will then be increased as it is the opinions of people of his own culture that become most important to him. This question was not systematically explored in the current study. However, it was marginally present in many interviews, and it seems clearly a significant factor. On the whole, it appeared that learning was encouraged by situations where the executive found his relationships in the company humanly satisfying so that his emotional ties with people out of the native culture were weakened.

These cases do not prove that direct criticism is always undesirable. There were cases observed in the research in which direct criticism had apparently been accepted with no bad side effects. All of these occurred between men whose relationships were already characterized by strong mutual respect. For example, Mr. Price had been in Mexico for many years and was the object of considerable admiration among his men. Mr. Farias, one of his staff men, was wont to develop new methods for other sections and then try to put them over by direct authority. Mr. Price told him that his methods were responsible for a lot of dissatisfaction and that it would be well if he spent more time trying to see each problem as the other people saw it and then try to suggest improvements which would make it better from their point of view. He hammered at this same line with Mr. Farias for many months; and, so far as one could determine, Mr. Farias did change; and his respect for Mr. Price was unimpaired.

This picture is too varied to permit generalizing. We can only observe that there are grave risks in attempts at direct criticism. Because of these risks, the experienced United States executives observed in this study favored indirect ways of communicating suggestions to subordinates along the lines to be discussed in the next chapter. While the techniques varied, the substance was much the same. The superior was making known to the subordinate the ideas in which he believed, but avoiding any direct clash with the subordinate's own attitudes. The subordinate, at least in an immediate sense, did not feel forced to accede to the new ideas; he could accept them or not without affecting his immediate relationship with the superior. It appeared from the research that under these conditions the individual would absorb a great deal.

Testing

The extent of actual learning is determined in the testing phase in which the individual tries out the new ideas, and determines their effectiveness for his purposes. To see what this testing process involves we can look again at the cases of Mr. Ortega, Mr. Fernandez and Mr. Carvajal. This discussion will again emphasize the conscious learning process, which is easier to observe. Essentially the same type of testing of an action-reaction nature is present in the unconscious process, as experienced, for example, by Mr. Carvajal over a period of years.

Mr. Ortega had absorbed intellectually a tremendous number of new management ideas. He tested them out in three ways. First, he used them in conversation, especially with his boss. Here he found they were valuable in getting approval, and he accordingly became accustomed to using their nomenclature instinctively at the right moments. Second, he tried them in practice in ways which did not affect his own personality. For example, he made a practice of keeping other department heads well informed about events in his department which affected them. This he also found valuable. It made a good impression on the boss and it resulted in a return flow of information from other departments and fewer difficulties in his operation. So, though it did not come naturally to him, he did on a routine basis a number of things which would be regarded as good communications. Third, he tried these ideas as part of his own, non-routine experience. That is, he experimented with them as a new way of life. Here he found them difficult and apparently useless. In meetings, for example, he occasionally volunteered an idea. As often as not this led to an argument with another man which accomplished nothing and, if the boss was there, resulted in an embarrassing appearance of lack of cooperation and evidence that one or the other of them did not know his job. Things went much more smoothly, and the boss was always more pleased, when he kept most of his thoughts to himself.

Mr. Fernandez tested his new ideas in the first instance by observing their success in the lives of other people. Therefore, when he tried them himself he was already strongly disposed to believe that they were good. He threw himself into applying them in practice in successively more complicated situations. In each case the results were rewarding in prestige, money and sense of accomplishment. By the time he reached his present job he was thoroughly convinced of the soundness of the ideas and they were quite deeply rooted in his own attitudes. In this job, however, these attitudes were being severely tested. Not only were his efforts to develop cooperative relationships meeting little success but there were indications that he could get ahead faster if he reverted to his former tough individualistic character. In fact, one could see in some of his relationships and attitudes that he was already moving in this direction.

Mr. Carvajal's testing process started at the level of pleasing the boss and placating the workers. He apparently accomplished both ends, but as other experiences came along he began to realize larger values from his methods. He saw that they resulted in people working harder, and above all, that he was receiving much appreciation and prestige from other people which made him feel important and useful. The potentialities of improving relationships all through the company became an exciting and rewarding objective in itself. So his testing advanced to a missionary-teaching stage and as he succeeded in that, the concepts became thoroughly imbedded in his own personality.

Each of these men had given new ideas a good testing and at the time they were observed, it appeared that the adjustments they had made in their own attitudes were a sound adjustment to the results of the testing process. Mr. Ortega was firmly fixed at the formal behavior level of change. In his particular situation it seemed likely that he would get further and be happier if he stayed as he was so far as basic attitudes were concerned. Mr. Fernandez had progressed a long way toward new attitudes, but he retained enough skill in his earlier ways so he could operate by them as needed. So long as he stayed where he was, such a degree of ambivalence seemed sound. Mr. Carvajal's attitudes were strongly established at the personal conduct level. The group around him were also either of the same sort, or moving in that direction, and he was able, therefore, to work very effectively following these attitudes.

The strong influence of the administrative atmosphere in changing the attitudes of executives which is evident in these cases was observed throughout my research. Since it is a factor which the United States executive can often affect significantly, it will be worthwhile to explore it in greater detail.

THE ADMINISTRATIVE ATMOSPHERE

Learning cannot take place out of context. People may learn some manual or simple intellectual skills independent of an environment. But administrative attitudes and actions are learned as part of the world in which the individual lives. These are fundamentals which will be readily accepted by most people. Our problem lies primarily in understanding what makes up the administrative atmosphere and how it affects foreign executives.

The elements of atmosphere which affect the individual executive most are those which are frequently felt in his own activities. These include his superiors and other men with whom he works regularly, and the patterns or systems by which the administrative group functions. To him, the most important elements of the atmosphere are those which affect the achievement of his personal objectives: advancement, praise, recognition, and work accomplishment.

The character of the atmosphere is determined primarily by actions, that is, the way in which individual members of the group act. Written procedures and other verbal expressions of administrative intentions have some relevance, but the character of the atmosphere is essentially determined by the actual performance of the individuals who compose the organization, especially that of the senior member.

Among the several organizations observed in this research there were significant differences which can best be discussed as contrasts between authoritarian and democratic atmospheres. In all of these organizations democratic patterns of administration were stated as objectives and were sought by various formal devices. For example, there was universal verbal encouragement of the free communication of ideas upward, and procedures such as committees and task groups were generally used as devices for collective decision-making. The real atmospheres, however, fell short of these objectives in varying degrees. In some cases, the responsible executives were conscious of this fact and regarded it as a sound adjustment to the realities of

life. In others, the extent of the differences between the real atmosphere and the objectives was not understood.

While none of the organizations could be classified as completely
authoritarian or completely democratic, a description of the two extremes based on a composite of characteristics found in various organizations will be illuminating.

In the authoritarian atmosphere the senior executive is a dominating individual. He feels that the organization is essentially *his*
organization. This attitude is passed on to others by a variety of actions. He takes full responsibility for the organization and assumes
unhesitating authority for all significant decisions. He encourages the
pyramiding of decision-making toward him. Above all, he fosters a
sense of personal dependence of subordinates upon him. He is liberal
with both praise and criticism, and subordinates are acutely conscious
of the importance of these evaluations. They therefore vie among
themselves for his favor. The subordinate's sense of accomplishment
is largely in terms of the opinion of the superior and his competitive
status vis-à-vis others in the organization.

In the democratic atmosphere the leader assumes what can best
be described as a residual responsibility as a member of the group,
though the term residual does not imply minor. The leader makes
decisions and takes actions which the group cannot handle, or which
it would handle much less effectively. For example, the leader selects
men for positions in the level immediately below him; he negotiates
on behalf of the group with his superiors; and he serves as arbitrator
when subordinates cannot reach a decision. He acts in all of these
matters with studied reluctance and thereby has a large measure of
support in what he does. For example, he does not assume the arbitrator role until the subordinates have exhausted their own capacities
for compromise and are prepared, therefore, to recognize the necessity for arbitration, if the work of the organization is to proceed. In
this system action is, for the most part, the result of collective decisions or of each individual working by himself in an area delegated
to him by common consent. (Actually the delegation is usually for-
malized by directives or regulations from above, but so far as the
atmosphere is concerned, the important factor is the general acceptance of the delegation.) In this atmosphere, the individual's ability
to achieve his ends depends primarily on his own ability to produce
in the area delegated to him and on his capacity to win the support
of his associates in common areas, as he can expect little support

from above if he is out of step with the group. His sense of accomplishment lies within himself as he measures what he has personally achieved, and with the group as he measures their support of his work in cooperative efforts.

As might be expected, the more democratic the atmosphere, the more encouragement is given to the development of group-oriented attitudes. This fact is fairly obvious and it, along with the United States ideological commitment to democratic principles, accounts for the common explicit endorsement of democratic organizational objectives. The problems observed in this research were not at the level of objectives but at the practical level of execution. At that level the typical United States executive was observed to have substantial difficulty accomplishing his objectives because of the need to develop an effective business organization with the realities of the personalities at hand, and because of the difficulty of recognizing the true character of the atmosphere of which he was himself a part.

To understand these problems we should start by observing that the extreme of the authoritarian organization described above was not a "bad" authoritarian system. It did not include any of the arbitrary or unfair or selfish characteristics which are commonly associated with dictatorships. These elements are not necessarily part of an authoritarian system. Because of the weaknesses of human nature and the personal power implicit in the system, they are often found in it. Thus, they are a risk but not an essential ingredient. In the partially authoritarian systems observed in this research, some degree of these characteristics could always be observed but it is not with them that we are immediately concerned. In the hands of an able executive a somewhat authoritarian system can be reasonably "good" or "clean," and it is that type of organization which we will consider.

Most of the Mexican executives observed in this study showed relatively strong individualistic tendencies. This is a reality around which the organizations had to be built. Specifically it meant that the capacities for cooperation of many men at lower levels was limited, so that, if decisions were to be reached on interdepartmental matters, they often had to be made by superiors. It meant that many subordinates did not report fully and frankly to superiors, so the superiors, to be reasonably informed, had to check quite thoroughly into aspects of operations down the line which might have been delegated. It also meant that the subordinates were so conscious of the role of superiors as a dominant factor in their lives, that to make them reasonably at ease in the company, the superior had to direct a good deal of praise and personal attention to them.

All of these actions create to a degree an authoritarian atmosphere. They are necessary as adjustments to the cultures of many foreign countries. If the business of a company is to move ahead, the organization must function, and it can function only if its systems are accommodated to the personalities of the personnel.

It is clear, however, that as the atmosphere becomes more authoritarian, the encouragement of group-oriented personality characteristics is reduced. Here then is the real problem of the United States executive. In the muddy area of somewhat authoritarian, somewhat democratic methods he has a certain degree of latitude which may permit more or less encouragement of change among his subordinates but still be consistent with the short-run and long-run effectiveness of the organization. Dealing with this problem in the dynamic processes of daily work is not easy, even when the nature of the situation is fully understood by the executive.

Unfortunately his life is complicated by two personality elements of which most of the overseas executives observed in this study did not seem sufficiently conscious. The first is the impact of business demands upon the authoritarian capacities of the United States executive. Most United States executives are very action-oriented. They want to be doing things, to get on with the job. They are also quite confident of the correctness of their own ideas and methods. Furthermore, they are under heavy pressure from the home office to "get results." The combined effect of these forces is to further the movement in the authoritarian direction. With variations, this picture was seen several times in my research and confirmed by reports from United States operations around the world. Surrounded by a group who are in many cases inferior to him in technical competence and are culturally inclined to submissiveness, the United States executive may become a strongly authoritarian boss. With a fairly small operation beneath him, he can personally keep track of all of its main activities and he assumes personal control of every significant phase of the work. He may be respected by his subordinates because in fairness and competence he is judged superior to other authoritarians they have known, but he is none the less an authoritarian. The immediate effectiveness of the business probably will be quite high, but there is little likelihood that the subordinates will be developing group-oriented attitudes.

The second problem is the difficulty of discerning the real character of the existing atmosphere. The United States executive is culturally inclined to put great faith in verbal reports. However sound this may be at home (which may be debated) it is a weakness abroad, especially in this area of interpersonal relations. If the executive talks about democratic organizational methods and tells his subordinates that he wants to develop them, he may be certain that the subordinates will also talk about them, most especially if they are astute individualistic types. He will hear a great deal from them about the cooperation they have given others, how they are developing their subordinates, and so forth. These reports may or may not be true depending on the men and the real tenor of the atmosphere which the United States executive has created. His knowledge of the atmosphere must depend on his ability to observe and understand his own actions and those of his subordinates.

Again I have stated these two problems in terms of extremes. For most United States executives, they do not appear that clearly. More often the problems are an accumulation of little incidents. To illustrate them we may consider a specific case. This case is unusual in that the problem is a possibility of retrogression of the atmosphere toward greater authoritarianism. More often the problem is what type of action will move towards a more democratic environment, but the essential elements are the same, and this case brings them out clearly.

Juan Raphael was the production manager of Elox Products, S. A., which made a variety of electrical appliances. One morning an assistant reported that a shaft in a machine which was essential to making one of the appliances had become slightly warped and he feared that, if it kept running that way, it would damage a bearing. If the bearing should break down suddenly, the whole machine might be damaged. Mr. Raphael inspected the machine and concluded that the best thing to do was to shut it down immediately and send for a new shaft from the United States. He figured that with air delivery he would get it in a week. He knew this would have an effect on the company's sales at a critical period so he called Mr. Ramirez, the sales manager. He told him a serious problem had developed and asked him to meet him in Mr. Putnam's office.

Mr. Putnam had been sent down six months previously as general manager. He had worked up through the sales organization in the United States and was considered likely material for higher general management positions. He had been assigned to Mexico as a means of giving him experience in over-all management in a small operation. He was very anxious to make a good record in Mexico as a step to his further progress in the company.

Mr. Raphael telephoned Mr. Putnam. He told him that the machine would probably have to be shut down and he would come up an explain it to him and Ramirez. Mr. Putnam preferred to see the machine first and went to the plant. His immediate reaction was that this was very unfortunate. It was then mid-fall, with demand at peak level in the Christmas build-up. Losing a week's production would be a serious blow to the company's sales. But he reserved comment until he had inspected the machine with Raphael. When the warping was pointed out to him, Mr. Putnam could see it but it looked very slight and it seemed unlikely to him that it could ruin the bearing. He expressed his doubts to Mr. Raphael, who replied that it was purely a matter of personal judgment. He thought there was a danger but there was no way to prove it at this point.

They returned to Mr. Putnam's office and wired for a new shaft and bearing which would be needed no matter what they decided. Mr. Ramirez was there when they arrived. Mr. Putnam explained what had happened and then said, "I think we should keep the machine going. It doesn't look really dangerous to me and it would hurt to lose a week's production. What do you think, Ramirez?" Mr. Ramirez said he agreed. Mr. Putnam turned to Mr. Raphael and said, "It looks like it's two against one. What do you say?" Mr. Raphael said he would leave the machine running for the rest of the day and he would like to think about it further. He returned to his office and commented to the observer approximately as follows:

"This is a tough one to deal with. You see, it is my right to determine if it is safe to operate a machine or not. In a decision like this it has to be my judgment which determines what we do. Mr. Putnam seems to have made up his mind. He wants to do it his way. Of course, I can see his concern. He's a salesman at heart. This is his first big season here and he wants it to be a good one. Then too, he's trying to learn how to be a general manager and that isn't easy. He's got to learn to understand production problems. He's been working at it hard since he came here. He spends a lot of time in the plant. He asks me questions and he has some good suggestions sometimes.

"Now this thing comes along. It's the first time we've had a big production problem that ran into sales. He thinks he's got some feel for machines and he thinks his judgment is sound. But that's something that comes to a man very slowly. I've been in production for years and I know a tremendous amount that he just can't expect to know after a few months. I know how much warp you can tolerate in a shaft. I've seen some go and I've seen some not go. You can't ever prove anything because shafts are all different—different sizes, speeds, and other things; but when a man lives with machines he gets a feel for them. I just have a feeling this one is going to go. I could be wrong but that's the way I feel.

"And this type of thing is my responsibility. Now, you can say that the general manager is responsible for the whole company, and that's true. But some things have to be delegated, and deciding when a machine is safe is one of the things that is delegated to the production manager. That is true in all Elox plants around the world. That's the way it has to be. You know a man has to have authority delegated to him. A man has to have room to work in or he can't get anything done. It's the general manager's responsibility all right, but he has to delegate it. If he doesn't trust me, he should fire me. I don't know what is going to happen on this. He does seem to feel pretty strongly about it. Maybe the best thing would be just to accidentally get one of the parts damaged so the machine couldn't run. I don't think I'll have to do that, though. He wouldn't force me to run it. It's a bad situation. Somehow things like this didn't happen when Mr. Finch was here."

To understand this story we need to know a little about Mr. Finch's methods. He had been the general manager for ten years prior to being sent to a larger branch. The men had admired his technical competence in the company's business, especially the production side. They had also liked him as a manager. He had always been helpful to them when they came to him with problems but he made a point of insisting that they make their own decisions. He directed the company's general policies with a firm hand, but the top management group apparently had a lot to say about the development of policies. When something came up it was usually discussed among them at lunch and in various formal and informal meetings. Sometimes the group would make a collective decision, and sometimes Mr. Finch would make the decision by himself, but his decision usually represented a consensus of their views.

While it is hard to predict such things, it is probable that under him the warped shaft problem would have been handled in another way. Mr. Raphael would probably have gone to him and Mr. Ramirez with the problem. Mr. Finch would have expressed uncertainty about the possible effect of a shutdown on sales. Mr. Ramirez would have given strong arguments about the amount of sales the company would lose. This would have troubled Mr. Raphael a good deal and he would have taken another look at the machine to check his own opinion. He might then have gone back to Mr. Finch, and they would have talked at some length about the problem. In the end Mr. Raphael might have said, "It sure is hard to know what to do. What would you do?" To this, Mr. Finch might have replied, "I really don't know. I suppose if I were in your shoes I'd shut it down. But then I'm not really in your shoes so I don't know."

Looking back at Mr. Raphael's actions, we can see an interesting contrast in attitudes. Most of them fit the pattern of the group-oriented personality, for example his sympathetic understanding of Mr. Putnam's situation and his instinctive talking over the problem with others. A few of them run in the individualistic direction—his protectiveness about his own authority and the suggestion that he might cripple the machine. The action of the general manager appears as the crucial factor in strengthening one or the other of these tendencies.

Mr. Finch's approach emphasized the man's personal authority, so that as problems were worked out the individual's position was not challenged and it did not become an issue in the solution which was reached. Mr. Putnam, by taking a strong position and then by his remark, "It's two against one," has clearly raised in Mr. Raphael's mind a threat to his authority and it has become a vital element in the subsequent action. For the moment Mr. Raphael is reassuring himself, "Deciding when a machine is safe is one of the things that is delegated to the production manager. That is true in all Elox plants around the world"; and, "He won't force me to run it." These are expressions of confidence in a system which was built up over ten years under Mr. Finch. There has been no overt change since Mr. Putnam arrived. There have been a few other incidents which have started Mr. Raphael wondering about Mr. Putnam's character, but he still has faith in the basic system.

This, then, is a turning point. If Mr. Putnam overrules him and as subsequent problems arise continues to draw authority toward himself, Mr. Raphael's individualistic tendencies will probably reassert themselves. It will then be clear to him that Mr. Putnam will be the dominant factor in all significant questions. He should therefore devote himself to getting in his favor so he will side with him when he has disputes with other department heads, and will give him approval when he wants to do things in his own department. In this orientation he will view Mr. Putnam and the other executives as essentially antagonists against his own domain, which will assume great importance to him.

This situation will contrast sharply with the atmosphere and feelings which had been developed as a result of Mr. Finch's leadership. As we saw, Mr. Raphael had a sense of confidence that others respected the privacy of his domain. He assumed he had a responsibility to talk over his problems with others when their departments were affected and to respect any reasonable opinions they presented. Therefore he did not in fact function independently, and the opinions of others influenced his work strongly. But he felt that the acceptance of these opinions was his own choice. He took considerable pride in this system as such. Working within the system he had made major accomplishments in which he took great personal pride.

SUMMARY

The dynamics of the Elox situation and the unfinished warped shaft story are a fitting end to this chapter. Other potential learning experiences could be described from the research and their immediate outcomes assessed. But we would gain little more from them than we can learn from the Elox case. The uniqueness of the business problems and individual personalities in each case would defy the development of specific rules to guide the conduct of the executive in new situations. The furthest we can go in the direction of useful generalizing is the understanding of the character of the learning process and the forces affecting it which have been outlined as this chapter progressed.

We have observed that the acceptance of new ideas as part of formal behavior is quite a different matter from absorbing them into one's personality as basic guides for personal conduct; and that adopting them into standards for the performance of others is a still different level of learning.

Two phases of the learning process were noted in which the United States executive had a significant influence. One was providing an initiative for change, a process which involved risks because of the potential irritation of sensitivities. The second was the testing phase in which the influence of the surrounding atmosphere was seen as the dominant factor. As the individual lives within a group, what he learns is what will be effective within that group in accomplishing his objectives in life. The actions and responses of his associates, and especially his superiors, are the answers to the testing process which are important to him in developing his attitudes.

~~~~~~

Chapter 6

The United States Executive Abroad

"How do they feel about me?" Probably every United States executive overseas has asked himself that question at least once. If he is sensitive at all he realizes that his position is conspicuous and unnatural. He is the foreigner, the strange object in the environment. His "foreign" associates are at home. Most of the things and people they see are a natural part of their environment. But he is not. He is thrust into their midst as an individual with differing ways, the agent of a foreign company and the emissary of a distant land. It is inevitable that he will arouse a variety of reactions and, if he is to be effective, he must understand the reactions and adjust his ways to make himself as acceptable as possible to his hosts.

ATTITUDES TOWARD UNITED STATES EXECUTIVES

On the whole, Americans abroad are viewed with a combination of confusion, awe and antagonism modified by a degree of generalized admiration and confidence. This situation is not a happy one, especially for a people with an over-riding desire to be liked. Still it is true. Whenever researchers cut through the surface gloss of foreign courtesy and diplomacy, they find these attitudes throughout foreign populations. My study reached the same conclusions as to feelings about United States executives, differing notably only in the great variations which existed in the attitudes toward specific individuals. Of these I shall say more at the end of the chapter because they provide useful insights into the things the executive may do to build good relationships. For the moment, however, we must consider the general attitudes. They are the starting point for each executive as he enters a new foreign assignment, and the feelings which created them are ever-present, ready to help or hinder him in his individual efforts to build bonds between himself and his associates.

Behind the general attitudes toward United States executives are a variety of forces, the most important of which can be grouped under four main headings: (1) cultural differences, (2) sensitivities, (3) attitudes toward the United States, and (4) effects of being a foreign executive in a United States company.

Enough has been said in earlier chapters about the first of these so that its significance need not be discussed at length. While in many cases United States cultural attitudes are admired and foreign executives seek to emulate them, they are still a source of stress. At best, they often put the foreign executive in an uncomfortable position where he must strain to adjust to new ways. At worst, they create difficult and frequently unpleasant situations of which we have seen a variety in the preceding chapters. In sum, they contribute to the general attitude that dealing with United States executives is likely to be an awkward, embarrassing, and confusing experience.

Sensitivities

The term "sensitivities" is used here to include feelings which affect the assurance, confidence and ease with which foreign executives approach their relations with United States executives. As many aspects of men's emotions come under such a broad heading, a psychological treatise would be required to cover it thoroughly. But I will discuss only a few characteristics which it appeared from the research were of most frequent importance in relations between United States and foreign executives.

Most significant among these characteristics is the degree to which the foreign executive feels secure and confident within himself. These quotations from varied sources spell out the nature of this problem.

> We have an inferiority here that everything is better there (outside India) than here. . . . I was upset and uneasy in the presence of an Englishman. . . . I had a deep-rooted inferiority

complex built on racial lines. . . . (Comments of three Indians)[1]
   The chief thing that I notice is that all the Mexicans have an inferiority complex when they're working with people from the States. (Observation of a United States executive)
   Above all, the Mexican suffers from a deep feeling of inferiority. . . . From these feelings of inferiority spring all his virtues and all his defects. (Analysis of a Mexican psychologist)[2]

The sensitivities described in these remarks vary from country to country. In Mexico, through a combination of circumstances, they are very strong. Most Mexican writers agree with Iturriaga that a feeling of inferiority and insecurity is fundamental to the Mexican national character. As to the origins of these feelings, there are a variety of explanations. Iturriaga feels the inferiority complex "has its roots in his [the Mexican's] colonial past, in his condition of a vanquished race, in the technical inferiority of his civilization vis-à-vis the conqueror, and in the fact that the racial mixture was fused not through love but through violence."[3] Samuel Ramos takes a similar historical viewpoint.[4] He starts with the initial impact of the subjugation of the Indian masses by the Spanish conquerors. During the colonial period the people were given very little chance to develop independent competence as individual efforts were typically beaten down, whether at the level of the Indian slave on the hacienda or the Mexican leader seeking national independence. When independence was achieved, a great period of frustration ensued. The Mexicans tried to project themselves quickly to European levels of democracy and standards of living. Over and over their efforts degenerated into political and economic chaos. Out of this experience, Ramos feels, came a deep sense of national inadequacy, a pervasive feeling that Mexicans were inherently incompetent by the standards of accomplishment set by other nations.
   Modern psychologists like Santiago Ramirez have been more concerned with the current family relationships as they affect the individual.[5] Because of the prevalence of the dual standard in Mexico, a young Mexican is likely to have an unsettling set of relations with

---

[1] John Useem and Ruth Hill Useem, *op. cit.,* p. 34.
[2] Jose E. Iturriaga, *op. cit.,* p. 229.
[3] *Loc. cit.*
[4] Samuel Ramos, *El Perfil del Hombre y la Cultura en México* (Mexico: Editorial Pedro Robredo, 1938), pp. 12–13.
[5] Santiago Ramirez, "Estructura Psicologica del Méxicano" (unpublished study), p. 5.

his parents and one or more maids. In the extreme case, he is the son of a man whose name his mother may not even know and whom he never sees. Somewhat less extreme and more common are the cases where the mother has a fairly regular relationship with the father, but in the child's upbringing the father is at best an infrequent friendly visitor and at worst, a harsh intruder. Most of the love and education the child receives come from the mother who, by virtue of her position, tends to be lonely and over-possessive. Most middle- and upper-class Mexicans derive from legal marriages but even in them the situation may not be much different, except that the stigma of illegitimacy is removed. If the father expends his time and love on another woman, he has limited contact with the children in his home, and that frequently of a disciplinary nature. The mother, again, is the major influence, though in upper- and middle-class homes her role may be largely assumed by the nursemaid.

Thus in Ramirez' view, regardless of the specific type of relationship, the female influence on the child is much greater than that of the father in early life. Then, because of the cult of masculinity (*machoism*), the maturing boy is forced to forsake the values of femininity and to a degree turn away from the individuals from whom he has received his satisfactions in childhood. The forces at work in the personality under these conditions are complex and beyond the scope of this book. We can readily accept, however, the conclusion of the Mexican psychologists that such a system will produce emotionally unstable individuals.

These historical and family influences have combined to foster feelings of inferiority and insecurity on a national scale. The executives observed in my research were not typical of their countrymen in this respect, because they were relatively ambitious and successful and had a considerable degree of self-confidence. In their working relations, however, many of them demonstrated a significant lack of emotional assurance. This lack of assurance was to some degree a part of their whole make-up, but it was notably present in relations with United States executives. Observing superior-subordinate relations, it was hard to separate this factor from the attitudes discussed in Chapter Four. Domineering on the part of superiors and submission by subordinates are the culturally-accepted patterns of behavior, and the lack of assurance leads naturally to similar actions. In many cases, however, there were feelings which went beyond what one would expect of simple submission to authority or the evasive submission of the determined, individualistic executive. For example, an executive who had done a good job on a particular project and had been promised a memorandum of commendation which would be sent to the home office, showed an almost obsessive concern when the memorandum was not forthcoming after a few days. Another man who had been promoted several times and was clearly doing a good job was seriously considering resigning because he felt his superior did not like him, a conclusion reached because the superior had told him twice that he did not like the way he had organized reports.

Similar feelings appeared in relations between United States and Mexican executives who, at least on the organization chart, were equals. While differences in age, jobs and abilities confused the picture, there was a general tendency for the Mexicans to be unduly deferential to United States executives on their own level and to be personally wounded by critical comments. In these and other cases it was evident that the men were insecure in their feelings about themselves and inclined at the slightest provocation to assume that the United States executives looked down on their abilities and did not respect them. There were men who were exceptions to this generalization, but even from them, emotional reactions would sometimes emerge which made one doubt that their self-confidence was as great as it usually appeared.

The underlying lack of personal assurance is the core of the national sensitivity problem in Mexico. Amplifying its effects are several other elements in Mexican life. First, there is the temperamental sensitivity of the Mexican. It is customary in studies of the Mexican personality to quote on this point the homicide rate of 38 per 100,000, the highest in the world, compared to 4.8 per 100,000 in the United States.[6] This statistic is hard to analyze because it also involves attitudes toward death, fatalism, and *machoism*. Doubtless, however, if there is something definable as "temperamentalism," then the Mexican is of a temperamental nature. His emotional responsiveness contributes to his artistic creativity and to the satisfactions he finds in living life to the hilt. But it also amplifies the impact of the feelings he is exposed to by the inferiority complex.

A second element which reinforces the inferiority complex of the individual Mexican in many cases is his limited training and competence. The current generation of Mexican executives are, by United

---

[6] *Economist,* August 17, 1957, p. 525.

States standards, undertrained for their jobs. The source of this problem is the extraordinary pace of Mexican economic development. Industrial production has been increasing at about 10 per cent per year for several years.[7] This expansion has required a tremendous number of executives. Yet in the 1930's and early 1940's training in business management scarcely existed and engineering education was on a limited scale. As a result, men have been drawn into management and pushed rapidly up the scale with a minimum of training and no time to learn much more than the bare essentials for their immediate jobs. Thus we might find the following as a typical comparison between United States and Mexican sales managers both responsible for sales of equal magnitude. The United States executive would be a graduate of college, with one year of graduate school and fifteen years as a salesman and branch office manager. The Mexican had left college when he was twenty, been hired as an assistant to the sales manager directly, and had become sales manager after six years in various head office jobs. The range of the United States executive's knowledge would be further broadened by frequent attendance at business club meetings and conventions, compared to the Mexican manager's attendance once a month at a recently-formed group of sales executives in Mexico City.

Most Mexican executives try to compensate for this lack of breadth of experience by reading magazines and studying textbooks, but frequently in their relations with United States executives they are conscious of their inadequacies. The fact that the demand for executives assures them of good jobs despite these shortcomings should be some comfort. But in the immediate interactions between individuals, that perspective is too remote to modify the executive's sensitivity.

A third aspect of the sensitivity problem is the discomfort of the individual in a strange situation. As we saw in Chapter Four, Mexican society is divided along class lines, and within classes there are fairly well-established patterns of conduct, many of them included in the concepts of *educacion* discussed in Chapter Two. The United States industrial organization does not fit this scheme. It encourages vertical

---

[7] In passing, I cannot help noting that Mexican accomplishments both in political and economic development in recent years are one of the outstanding bright spots in a troubled world. Why the inferiority complex persists is hard to understand. It does, though, and we are concerned with what "is," not what "should be" and, I suspect, "will be."

mobility and it has its own code of social relationships, calling for greater informality and free-speaking.

The individual Mexican executive in this new environment may or may not be at ease. Those who find their abilities move them economically, and thereby socially, higher than their initial status may find it hard to conduct themselves with others, especially Mexicans who were born to higher classes. More common are the problems of readjusting to the social codes of a United States executive group. Such an apparently simple thing as being addressed by one's first name can be a trying experience for a Mexican. In Mexican society that intimacy is usually reserved for the closest friends or certain superior-subordinate relationships. Men who are unfamiliar with United States social practices and are relatively inflexible in their attitudes are likely to be very sensitive in their interactions with United States executives, anxious to please and yet unsure or awkward in meeting situations as they arise.

Sensitivities of a similar nature often complicate relations between United States executives and senior foreign businessmen. This was one of the factors contributing to the problems John Macy was encountering in dealing with Vishnu Rama in the situation described in Chapter One. Mr. Macy was an able young man and in the United States he was accustomed to negotiating on equal terms with men of greater age and titular stature. In Indian society young men are rarely accorded such respect. Typically, they are expected to keep their opinions to themselves. Mr. Rama was offended by the whole idea of a brash young man questioning his methods of running his business. His attitude would apply as well in Mexico and most foreign countries.

In the nature of the way United States companies manage their foreign operations, situations of this character occur all too frequently. Relatively young executives are typically given substantial responsibility for developing business abroad. Because authority in local companies is generally in the hands of older men, frequently of high social status, the United States executives often find themselves thrust into relationships which are offensive to the dignity of the local businessmen. Relations with high government officials result in similar incongruous and uncomfortable situations. As noted in Chapter Four, United States businessmen overseas are generally accepted into circles above their social and economic background, the typical middle-class United States executive finding fairly ready acceptance among upper-class foreigners. By the same token senior foreign executives are somewhat more tolerant of young United States executives than of young men of their own nationality. Nonetheless, there are limits to their tolerance and one hears numerous critical comments from foreigners about the character of the men United States companies send abroad to do business with them.

Recognition of this problem is one of the characteristics of many companies which have been successful in their business relationships abroad. These companies make a practice of dispatching senior men overseas to handle important negotiations, and many of them employ local nationals of significant social stature to conduct affairs which involve senior local businessmen. The younger United States executives are still used to handle the bulk of the work and detailed negotiations, but the presence of men who carry titles and an air of high authority creates an atmosphere of mutual respect which puts local businessmen and government officials in a receptive mood.

Finally, I should mention a very basic source of sensitivity. Mexican life is undergoing tremendous changes and in the process shaking every aspect of the culture. Just what this may mean for each individual is hard to say. The younger and more aggressive Mexicans who are the type who become executives frequently feel they are out in front of their countrymen.[8] There must be an exhilaration for the individual in this situation but there must also be problems in the uncertainties accompanying the loss of established roots and the evolution of new values. The dimensions of the potential problems are evident in the analyses of the impact of changing societies on the individual by Elton Mayo[9] and others.

This study did not explore the subject, but it did produce little items which suggest the type of problem which may trouble the Mexican executive. For example, there were several executives looking ahead to retirement with major worries, as they saw the established pattern of the younger generation caring for the old disappearing, and there were men who were concerned by the impact of greater activities by their wives, even to the point of working. These items do not add up to any conclusion but they do suggest one more element which contributes to the sensitivities of the Mexican executive.

It is difficult to summarize this section because of the wide variations

[8] Ralph L. Beals and Norman D. Humphrey, *op. cit.*, p. 11.
[9] Elton Mayo, *op. cit.*, pp. 117-137.

of sensitivities in individuals and the differences in the effects of their feelings on their attitudes toward United States executives. One can only observe that there are these varied sources of potential insecurity which result in sensitivities among Mexicans and make it hard for them to have easy relations with all people, and especially United States executives. The Mexican situation in this respect appears to be quite extreme. In some countries, notably the mature, independent nations of Europe, sensitivities of this character are not a significant problem. However, in most of the underdeveloped countries, especially those which have gone through extended periods of colonial domination, feelings of inferiority and insecurity similar to those found in Mexico are common.

Attitudes toward the United States

What do foreigners think about our country? To the typical United States citizen the United States appears as a bulwark of peace and democracy and a great productive system which has brought wealth to all its people while giving generously to help other countries. If ever a nation deserved love and respect, it should be the United States. Whatever the merits of this view may be, it is only partially shared by foreigners. One needs only to read the newspapers to know that. From a number of extensive studies we have a realistic picture of what various peoples do think of us.[10] A measure of love and respect are found, but equally important are significant fears, a good deal of envy, and some real doubts about the quality of our culture.

In Mexico, all of these views are present, adding up to one underlying emotional attitude. As Beals and Humphrey observe, "If one can probe deeply enough below the heavy armor of courtesy, virtually every Mexican reveals a significant amount of anti-American feelings." [11] Today those feelings on a national scale are dormant after erupting violently in the expropriation of the oil properties in 1938. But at times they seem close to boiling over again, as in 1956, when the mismanagement of a study of technical educational programs in Mexico led to student strikes and violence against the United States university group working on the project.

[10] "America through Foreign Eyes," *The Annals* (Philadelphia: The American Academy of Political and Social Science), September, 1954, Volume 295.
[11] Ralph L. Beals and Norman D. Humphrey, *op. cit.,* pp. 47–48.

The basic anti-United States attitude is the cumulative result of many events and probably will persist for a long time to come. It dates back at least to the capture of Mexico City by the United States Marines in 1847. Second only in size to the monuments to the Independence and the Revolution is the memorial to Mexico's child heroes, the six boy cadets who died defending Chapultepec Castle from the United States invaders. It has served for many years to remind Mexicans of the dangerous might of the nation to the north, and unfortunately there have been more vivid reminders within the memory of current leaders—the seizure of Vera Cruz by the United States Navy in 1914 and the Pershing raids after Pancho Villa in northern Mexico in 1917.

Direct military invasion from the United States is so unlikely today that few Mexicans are concerned about it. Their attitudes about direct relations with the United States in the political field are now relatively confident. There is, however, a deep sense of concern, especially among educated people, about their helplessness in world affairs. People in the United States may be worried about the threat of war, but at least we know that through our diplomats and military forces we can make many efforts to stave off the threat. The Mexicans, along with practically every other nation in the world, are in a quite different position. They can do little but stand on the sidelines and let the giants thrash out their differences. But they fully expect that when trouble comes they will be deeply involved. In this helpless position they are irritated by some United States policies, which they feel are more likely to increase than decrease world tensions.

In the economic sphere Mexican fears about the United States are more specific. The United States is viewed as bent on a road to economic imperialism which sets it at cross purposes with Mexico's national ambitions. A striking manifestation of this feeling is the lengthy introduction to *La Industrializacion de Mexico* by Manuel German Parra.[12] Dr. Parra was the personal economic adviser to Presidents Aleman (1946–52) and Ruiz Cortines (1952–58), and his words may be taken as representative of both political and intellectual opinion. His book is written to defend Mexico's policy of rapid industrialization and answer the arguments of Frank Tannenbaum who, in his book, *Mexico, the Struggle for Peace and Bread,* advocated con-

[12] Manuel German Parra, *La Industrializacion de México* (Mexico: Imprenta Universitaria, 1954).

tinued agrarian development and slow industrialization.[13] In his introduction Dr. Parra takes pains to relate Tannenbaum's views to the schemes of United States capitalists to prevent Mexican industrialization and keep Mexico as a source of cheap raw materials and a market for United States manufactured goods. A brief quotation shows the tenor of his sentiments.

> The theory of Professor Tannenbaum served so adequately the great interests of foreign manufacturers, fearful of losing their markets in the Latin American nations, that it was very quickly converted into a popular thesis. The editorial pages of the most influential publications of the neighboring country were filled with disinterested warnings about the terrible danger that we were running if we insisted on industrialization.[14]

This general apprehension is bolstered by specific United States policies which hurt Mexico, such as the cotton surplus disposal program and the threat of high lead and zinc tariffs. To the typical United States citizen the tariff issue is a minor matter, but to Mexico it is a major worry. Minerals compose 20 per cent of the country's exports, and a significant loss of exports means a cut back in imports, most of which are machinery and equipment for the industrialization program.

It is beyond the scope of this book to explore all of the problems of United States Mexican economic relations. Obviously there is much to be said on each side of the argument. Our concern here, however, is not with the rights and wrongs of the policies but with the attitudes which they engender in Mexicans. Some United States policies, especially development loans, stimulate Mexican appreciation, but a great many reinforce the latent feelings of distrust and dislike. Unfortunately it is the latter which receive the greatest publicity and the effect is a general conception of the United States as an antagonist, not a friend, in economic affairs. This type of attitude is found in every part of the world, for United States trade and investment policies conflict in some way or other with the objectives of most countries, creating widespread fears of United States economic imperialism.

The other major source of negative feelings about the United States is on a different plane, that of culture and character. On the basis of

[13] Frank Tannenbaum, *Mexico, the Struggle for Peace and Bread* (New York: Knopf, 1950).
[14] Manuel German Parra, *op. cit.*, p. 11.

a broad study of Mexican opinions, one observer sums up the prevalent attitude: "Educated persons who have not been in the United States often view Americans as crass materialists—engineers or businessmen —wealthy yet eager for money and quite devoid of culture in its highest sense." [15] This is a view which is common around the globe. Some people feel it is in part a defense mechanism of those who, unable to match United States standards of material wealth, take refuge in assertion of their own cultural superiority. However, especially to a stranger, the United States culture can readily be judged critically on this count. The Mexican executive seems less inclined to such attitudes, being himself of a materialistic bent, but they crop up from time to time in individual situations and undoubtedly are an unconscious part of the general attitude of the Mexicans toward United States executives.

Partially offsetting these specific negative feelings in the political, economic and cultural spheres are some rather diffused positive attitudes about the United States and its people. Above all, the United States is respected for its democracy. While the racial discrimination issue takes the edge off our glory, the United States is still seen as a land of real equality in political rights and economic opportunity. Its standards in these fields are widely admired and they set the goals for people striving for a better life in many lands.

Second, Americans are liked for their openness and generosity. In a broad opinion study one researcher found that the "big heart" theme ranked with respect for United States power, wealth and technology as dominant in the attitudes of foreigners concerning the United States.[16] The gum-dispensing G.I., the photo-snapping tourist and the zealous foreign-aid technician may not be ideal diplomatic representatives, but the net response to the mass of Americans, who have by now touched practically every part of the world and to the tremendous outpouring of United States economic aid has been favorable. People almost everywhere sense that the United States is generally good and her people are friendly and trustworthy.

These two great positive feelings, along with the general respect for

---

[15] Norman D. Humphrey, "The Mexican Image of Americans," *The Annals* (Philadelphia: The Academy of Political and Social Science), September, 1954, p. 116.
[16] Arvid Brodersen, "Themes in the Interpretation of America by Prominent Visitors from Abroad," *The Annals* (Philadelphia: The American Academy of Political and Social Science), September, 1954, p. 31.

United States industrial skill and wealth, go a long way to counteract the specific negative attitudes. The result in relations, both between nations and individuals, is a general milieu of confidence, through which misunderstandings and disputes arising from specific areas of distrust and disagreements break with easy provocation.

The Effect of Being a Foreign Executive in a United States Company

No one wants to be a second class citizen, least of all an ambitious business executive. Yet that, to a greater or lesser degree, is the status of virtually all foreign executives in United States companies. And because their status is based on the comparative position of the United States executives, their reactions are quite naturally directed toward them as well as toward the company policies which are the real determinants of their position.

The feelings of the foreign executive arise for the most part from two types of policies: selection of men for senior jobs, and compensation. The policies of United States companies on the first of these differ widely. In some, foreign executives are excluded from the top levels of the organization while in others, United States executives hold only a limited number of key jobs and even these are said to be open to foreign executives when their competence is established. In a very few instances the top positions are actually occupied by local nationals. The over-all soundness of the restrictive policies of most companies can be argued at length but their effect on the feelings of the foreign executives is quite' clear. They resent any sort of discrimination. To them it is both a matter of national pride and a block to personal ambition.

My research was concentrated in companies which were especially progressive in advancing foreign executives. Many of the Mexican executives in these companies had worked for less progressive companies and at times they became quite emotional about the discrimination they had experienced. Likewise, most of them were appreciative of the opportunities they now had, but, as the ambition of men is often insatiable, even among them resentment could be found. Inevitably the more able and ambitious Mexicans are attracted to the companies whose promotion policies are most favorable. In all but a very few of these there is home office reluctance to yield the last few top posts to local nationals. Thus there almost always comes a point where the Mexican finds his advancement checked, and regardless of the favorable character of the policies which have raised him to that level, a degree of resentment arises from the block to future progress.

Compensation policies are more uniform among companies, or at least there are few which are not clearly discriminatory in the eyes of foreign executives. In order to attract United States executives abroad, compensation in excess of United States salaries is usually needed. That is not so true in choice assignments like Mexico, but even there it applies to some extent. And for hardship posts, companies generally provide very substantial compensation. This practice, combined with the generally lower salary scales in foreign countries, results in differentials between United States and foreign executives in similar jobs. The United States executive may burn up his extra pay in sending his children home for schooling and other costs the national does not carry. But the foreign executive either does not see these things or does not see them the same way. After all, why shouldn't he also be able to send his children to the United States? To him it is essentially the issue of equal pay for equal work.

To the discrimination in salaries are usually added differences in fringe benefits, of which pensions loom most prominently in the minds of the foreign executive. Pensions for United States executives in foreign assignments are typically handled by the same system as for domestic personnel. But United States companies are only now beginning to develop pension systems for their foreign executives. In view of the small group of executives employed in each country, the undeveloped financial systems in many countries, and other complications, there are real problems of evolving such systems. But again, however, the foreign executive is concerned with the fact, not the reasons behind it.

The remarks of one Mexican executive portray vividly the impact of these policies. This executive, Mr. Vianos, had been in his present job for five years. Three United States executives had held the next higher job during that period, the third, Mr. Black, having arrived six weeks before this conversation. According to company policies, the superior job was open to local nationals but Mr. Vianos had reached the conclusion that in practice this was not true.

"I'm not sure if I'll stay with the company or not. There is nothing more for me here. I don't think it is fair the way things are done. I can't see any basis for sending a man down here like Mr. Black. He's sent down here with a big salary. But what is he worth? He has no contacts, he knows nothing about Mexico, he really has nothing much to contribute. It is all decided in the home office, and they don't understand the situation in the foreign units. They come down on their flying trips and talk to the top men, Mr. Pitts [the general manager], Mr. Calhoun [the assistant general manager], and Mr. Black. How can they hope to know anything about the organization? They don't understand our problems. They don't know how hard it is for the Mexicans to make ends meet. They talk about the financial problems of the men from the States, but we have ours here, too. This pension business, for example. Our people really worry about that. I'm O.K., perhaps, but for the older men this is a real worry. It used to be that a man could expect his sons to look after him when he got old. But now that's changing. Children are more independent now. They want to use their money for their own lives. A man doesn't feel good about these things. I'm going to stick it out for a while. I'm still not sure about Mr. Black. If he's nice to work with maybe I'll stay."

Mr. Black, of course, was not responsible for this situation, but he was an obvious target. Mr. Vianos was disappointed at not being promoted. He had a strong feeling that the home office was not giving him a fair deal, and he regarded Mr. Black, the latest arrival from the States, as the symbol and advocate of those policies. If he was to have a satisfactory relationship with Mr. Vianos, Mr. Black had his work cut out for him.

Summary

This discussion has emphasized the negative side of the picture, the forces which foster antagonism, dislike or insecurity in the feelings of foreigners toward United States executives. There are compensating forces which help develop easier relationships. Notable among them, especially in the case of Mexico, is the instinctive friendliness of the people toward strangers. This characteristic may seem inconsistent with the nature of the individualistic personality described in Chapter Two, but it is common throughout the population. Mexicans of all classes usually show a helpfulness and friendliness to tourists and business visitors which goes quite beyond the bounds of simple courtesy and the formalities required by *educacion*. In addition, we have noted already the generalized respect for United States democracy and standards of fair and egalitarian personal conduct.

In emphasizing the negative side, I did not intend to discount these positive elements. It seemed more important to talk about the negative aspects, however, for two reasons. The first is the difficulty of perceiving them, which will be the subject of the next section. The second is that on the whole they are more strongly held and more personal than the positive feelings. The issues which cultural differences can raise are of daily importance in executive relationships. The sensitivities of the foreign executive are exposed nerves, ready to twitch at any provocation. The anti-United States feelings are strong prejudices always in the background waiting to magnify specific issues. And the sense of discrimination is a constant corroding element in a man's attitude toward the company and the executives from the United States.

THE FACADE

The picture I have painted of the feelings of foreign executives is hard to believe as one watches them at work. In relations with their United States associates, they usually appear reserved but friendly and cooperative. This appearance presents a baffling problem for the United States executive. It is quite possible that it is a valid expression of feelings. We have seen that there are foreign executives who are competent and secure, and who are open and outgoing in their relations with others. The words of these men can generally be taken at face value. What negative feelings they have they will usually state quite freely.

But such frankness is rare, even among men with relatively open personalities. This is not unique to foreign cultures. In the United States ideological value is attached to a man's frankness in telling his superior how he feels. But in practice subordinates show considerable reserve. It may be heroic to bare one's soul to the boss but it is often wiser to hold one's tongue. This tactical reticence is amplified abroad by the character of men's feelings and the cultural attitudes toward relationships.

The feelings we have considered are not of the individual variety which concern the typical United States subordinate, e.g., resentment over the superior's promotion decisions or a feeling that the boss is a "credit grabber." These are specific issues which are within the control of both men. The subordinate may feel it is wiser to hold his peace; or, if he does speak out, he may often receive the support of others of his superiors, since his boss, in cases like those I have mentioned, is likely to be breaking the codes of our national culture. Feelings like these exist in relations between United States and foreign executives and they complicate the picture. However, they are not the same type of feelings as those we have been discussing. Reactions against cultural differences in administrative concepts, sensitivities fostered by a national inferiority complex, anti-United States attitudes, and resentment at discrimination against foreign executives are feelings that run deep in a man's system. In most cases they cannot be resolved by changes in the immediate situation. The particular executives who may be at hand are just small parts of the total situation which created the feelings. Company policies and forces permeating the society around the men are the real controlling factors. Where feelings arise from some immediate issue, a subordinate may feel that if he just "takes the bull by the horns," he can straighten it out. But how can the foreign executive hope to straighten out problems of this order? In some cases he cannot even understand their character, and in all of them change based on one man's effort seems hopeless.

Reinforcing this feeling are cultural attitudes toward superiors and the circumstances of life. The essence of the attitude of the subordinate in the authoritarian society is acceptance and submission. As we saw in Chapter Two, this attitude is prevalent in foreign cultures. Its effect on the inclination of the subordinate to express any negative feelings toward the superior is obvious. He just does not do it. And this applies even among men who are relatively free-speaking. In this research I observed a number of men who, on the whole, were frank in communicating their opinions about business matters to their superiors. Only one of these was apparently willing to stand up to a United States superior and tell him quite freely how he felt on more sensitive matters. He had done it once on a ticklish problem of internal relationships and probably would again. But as one might expect, this individual harbored very few negative feelings anyway.

By and large the picture was a consistent one: negative feelings of varying character and intensity all well hidden behind a facade of amenability and courtesy. Maintaining the facade is, of course, just an extension of the general attitude of "dealing with" the superior described in Chapter Two. The values and conditioning of the culture prepare the individual for just this role. In his early training the emphasis on *educacion,* or its equivalent in other societies, accustoms him to skill in speaking and acting according to an approved pattern which runs counter to any expressions of inner resentment, rebellion, or insecurity he may feel. He comes to maturity astute in the art of keeping to himself his attitudes toward people and appearing to them according to the model which he supposes they desire.

The character of the facade each executive constructs varies according to the United States executive he is dealing with. The facades observed in this research had certain fairly common characteristics, however. In the question of cultural differences in administrative methods, most of the foreign executives verbally accepted, and in practice applied to a degree the concepts of the superior (the formal behavior phase of learning, Chapter Five). Sensitivities were hidden behind a mask of reserve and apparent lack of feeling. Anti-United States feelings were camouflaged by silence mixed with acceptance of the anti-United States comments which most United States executives will volunteer, and admiration for United States industrial superiority, which is sincere. Feelings about discrimination against foreign executives were hinted at but rarely expressed.

PATTERNS OF ACTION BY UNITED STATES EXECUTIVES

The facade confronts the United States executive with a perplexing problem. How is he to adjust himself to the feelings of the foreign executive if those feelings are hidden from him? That is a hard question to answer, but not a hopeless one. We may start by taking heart in the fact that many United States executives are effective in this regard. With some, their adjustments may be pure instinct or luck. Others appear, however, to have made a deliberate effort to think out the problem before them and to adopt patterns of action which minimize the active or potential negative attitudes of the foreign executives. From these patterns some useful ideas may be distilled.

The actions of effective United States executives are related to the thoughts which have been developed in this chapter. Among the issues already discussed are the seeds of serious personal antagonism between United States and foreign executives. The antagonism may or may not be serious at the outset of a relationship, but it can readily be built up in the absence of positive forces in the other direction. The essence of the conduct of the successful United States executive is the construction of strong personal bonds which overcome the risks in the background. The individual executive cannot hope to change appreciably the basic sources of the negative feelings of the foreign executive. He is able, however, to establish a relationship in which these basic feelings are ineffective.

What does this mean specifically? As always, generalizations are dangerous, but in the next few pages certain patterns of action will be noted which cropped up frequently during the research and evidently made for better relations.

Direct versus Indirect Communication

The United States ideological values in favor of frankness have been mentioned already. In practice frankness is often restricted in upward communication. In downward communication, however, it is common, being essential to important phases of management, such as executive evaluation systems. The boss is supposed to tell the subordinate exactly where he stands, what is wrong with him, and how to improve himself.

Foreign cultures which tend to be more authoritarian are confusing on this point. Whereas upward communication is sharply restricted, there is little limitation on what may be said downward. Superiors can and do tell their subordinates just as much as in a democratic system. The confusion arises as a result of differences in objectives. The authoritarian is primarily concerned with obedience. Whatever love and respect subordinates have for him arise from the security and benefits which he bestows on them. Subordinates do not like criticism, but it is accepted as the price they pay for being subordinates.

The United States executive usually does not wish to develop this sort of relationship. There may be something to be said for "a good clean dictatorship," but as a practical matter the typical United States executive does not believe in authoritarianism, and his early training does not equip him to be effective in its application. While he requires a degree of discipline and obedience of subordinates, his objective is to elicit a high degree of voluntary effort in company work and self-improvement; and this he feels will be fostered, if the subordinate appreciates him and likes him as a person.

In seeking this objective we find that democratic frankness causes trouble. Subordinates conditioned to the practices of authoritarian cultures interpret it by their own standards and they resent it. Humphrey, in his general study of Mexican attitudes toward the United States, found this to be a common cause of difficulty. "The forthrightness of the American offends the *dignidad* of the Mexican peasant or urban worker, as well as the intellectual." [17] In my research it cropped up frequently and in discussing their operating codes, effective United States executives recognized its significance with such statements as: "The Mexicans just can't take direct criticism," or "I avoid laying it on the line as much as I can."

Taken by themselves these statements are inaccurate, for under authoritarian superiors, Mexicans have been "taking direct criticism" for centuries. Offense to *dignidad* has been commonplace in the traditional Mexican culture. However, they cannot take criticism *and* respond to it as part of a democratic context. Their tendency is to hear it and react to it by the patterns of the authoritarian system. The words of the superior are understood to be unilateral dictates rather than one side of a democratic process of exchanging views. Accordingly the subordinate is offended and reacts covertly and defensively, so that the frankness of the superior is destructive of the freedom in communication which he is attempting to build. A brief case will illustrate the problems which can ensue.

Ralph Hughes was sent to Mexico as general manager of the Kew Company. He was an able, straightforward engineer who had come up through the domestic production organization. When he arrived in Mexico, he found a number of things about the factory operation which he thought could be improved. He had great respect for Mr. Trevino, the production manager, but he did not think his approach was good on these points. As was his practice, he told Mr. Trevino exactly what he thought was wrong. He assumed Mr. Trevino might disagree with him and he was prepared to admit he was wrong if Mr. Trevino had a good argument. He was surprised when Mr. Trevino accepted all his criticisms with only a few minor objections. He concluded that Trevino was a very alert and amenable fellow who was going to be a good man to work with.

Mr. Trevino, meantime, was deeply troubled by this experience, his first significant encounter with the new manager. He came to the conclusion that if Mr. Hughes was displeased with so many aspects of his work, it must be that he did not like him and he was prepared to resign. Fortunately, he talked with Mr. Smith, the sales manager, who was also from the United States but had been in Mexico for several years. Mr. Smith expressed some surprise because he said Mr.

[17] Norman D. Humphrey, *op. cit.*, p. 117.

Hughes had spoken very highly of Mr. Trevino. That same day Mr. Smith talked with Mr. Hughes, who was equally surprised. Characteristically, Mr. Hughes called Mr. Trevino right in and reported his conversation with Mr. Smith. Then he explained that he considered Mr. Trevino a fine production manager and his criticisms were just his way of doing things. Eventually the two reached a *modus operandi* and were able to work well together. Mr. Trevino, however, was a rather exceptional man. He would fit the classification of a group-oriented personality and was more secure and out-going than most Mexican executives. Other cases were observed where criticism offended a subordinate, and unexpressed feelings of antagonism and lack of appreciation made for quite poor relations; and cases were reported to me of individuals who were so disturbed by criticism that they quit, as Mr. Trevino probably would have, but for Mr. Smith's presence.

All of this does not mean that direct criticism is impossible. Between some individuals, especially where the relationship has been built on a firm basis over an extended period, it is both possible and desirable. Rather, it means that the risks are relatively high. On the basis of this research, I would say that even experienced executives typically underestimate these risks. For example, in one apparently well-established relationship, critical pressure on an operating problem unnerved a Mexican executive to the point of making several unwise decisions. His closeness to the superior seemed noticeably shaken after the incident.

So we start with a negative point, the avoidance of direct criticisms or challenges which stir up the resentment or insecurity of the foreign executive. But this sounds impractical. After all, there is business to be done, and, if subordinates are to be taught to do a good job, they must know when they do poorly and how they may improve. That is perfectly true but more needs to be said to complete the story.

The point is not that subordinates should not be told when they do poorly, but rather that there are better ways to tell them than direct criticism. Though they are varied in nature, all of these ways may be loosely grouped under the heading of indirect communication, that is, the transmission of an idea without stating it explicitly to the individual. Among the specific methods are setting an example, talking about desirable methods in the abstract, and commending the work of those who do what is desired so that others hear about it.

Such methods of communication are not uncommon in the United

States. They assume greater importance in Mexico and many other cultures, however, for two complementary reasons. The first is the difficulty of direct communication on sensitive subjects. These difficulties extend throughout the population because of the sensitivities discussed earlier in the chapter and the tendency toward emotional patterns of action discussed in Chapter Three. Remember the homicide rate. There is a strong inclination among the people to seek indirect ways of communication which reduce the tensions and risks created by direct approaches. In Mexico, this inclination is well established in the use of the *indirecta* as the proper way to transmit critical opinions.

The second reason is that, at least in dealing with superiors, the people are more sensitive to indirect communications. This is but one phase of the basic authoritarian superior-subordinate relation. The subordinate is, in the vernacular, "tuned in" on the superior. He devotes himself assiduously to analyzing the superior's words and ways. He is alert for every hint as to the boss's desires. If praise is going to another man and not to him, he will have no trouble knowing that the boss is not pleased. If the boss calls him in and talks in general terms about the importance of delegation, he will worry about whether he is delegating properly.

So communicating indirectly with the sensitive individual does not appear to be difficult. The Mexican executives observed in this study seemed to understand quite well what their superiors thought regardless of the methods of communication the superior used. Whether they will, in fact, meet the boss's wishes is another matter. That depends upon the attitudes discussed in Chapters Two and Five. Our concern here, however, is with the effect of the communication on the feelings of the foreign executive toward the United States executive. On the whole, it appears that whereas direct critical communication can create antagonism or dislike, indirect communications at least do no harm and, to the extent that the foreign executive observes that his feelings are being respected, they may actually help the relationship.

Simpatico

As this study progressed various people observed that the main task would be arriving at a real understanding of the implications of being *simpatico*. Actually there was a good deal more to the study, but exploring the meaning of *simpatico* did prove a useful piece of work, providing some interesting insights into the Latin American character. Practically everyone in the United States seems to know that *simpatico* is used by Latin Americans to designate people of whom they approve. Because of the similarity in the words and because of their own cultural standards, there is a tendency for the North American to equate *simpatico* with sympathetic. This is an erroneous oversimplification. The sympathetic individual is one who shares the joys and sorrows of others in an understanding way. Such an individual may or may not be *simpatico*.

The dictionary definitions of *simpatico* are not too helpful as they concentrate on the "proper" meaning of words rather than their use in the vernacular. A leading Spanish dictionary defines *simpatico* as expressing a "relationship between two organisms such that when one suffers an ailment, the other experiences it also." This is essentially the basic meaning of sympathy, and since they share the same Latin root, it is natural that they should be initially similar.

The most widely used Spanish-English dictionary is more helpful because it attempts to include everyday usages of words in Latin America as well as basic Spanish meanings. For *simpatico* it gives "sympathetic, congenial; pleasant, agreeable, nice." The semicolon is significant. The first definition is the basic one. The second is recognized as something distinguishably different, and as a part of general usage.

The way in which people actually use the word is the best indication of its meaning. Here are two brief stories which are representative of its usage by most Mexicans.

At a party a middle-aged man dominated the conversation. His comments were witty and forceful. He dealt with the remarks of others deftly and showed little interest in answering helpfully a few questions which came to him. The following day a younger Mexican was loud in his praise of the man. "Senor X is so wonderful. He always knows just the right things to say. He's so brilliant. The party never gets dull when he is there. He is very *simpatico*." Another young man spoke approvingly of a superior. "He's a fine fellow. He's always got something interesting to say. When we go to the club he knows just how to talk to the waiters and just what to order. He is really *simpatico*."

The emphasis in these incidents is on the second part of the dictionary definition, and the first part does not seem to be relevant. To the typical Mexican a man is *simpatico* if he makes life pleasant. It is not necessary for him to show an interest in the problems of others. In fact, Mr. X was clearly not interested. He was neither a listener nor a sympathizer.

This point seems quite important. The United States executive who wants to win the accolade of being called *simpatico* need not be too concerned about being sympathetic. The Mexican does not necessarily dislike the sympathetic individual, but there are reasons to doubt that being sympathetic will help one's *simpatico* rating. The attitudes of the individualistic personality do not encourage that sort of relationship.

A comparative stranger who tries to achieve great intimacy and who pries into personal worries and problems is a threat to the security of the individualistic personality. Two Mexican executives stated flatly that they thought United States executives should not try to get familiar with the Mexicans they worked with, at least not till they had known them for some time. This did not mean that they did not want to have their superiors interested in them. But watching the United States executives who seemed most successful, it is clear that there is a fine line between being responsible for and concerned about your men and yet respecting the privacy of their lives. Such a line also exists in the United States, but with the Mexican the area of privacy is typically broader. The man who is *simpatico* has a good sense of where this line is.

The contrast between sympathetic and *simpatico* is also found in the levels of personality they describe. We usually think of sympathy as coming from the heart; it is a quality of a man's inner character. It involves feelings and the communication of feelings. *Simpatico*, however, describes little more than superficial manner. A man may be hard-hearted, or deceitful, or unsympathetic and still be *simpatico*. He may give orders to subordinates which they do not like, or be unduly critical, and still be *simpatico*. The only requirement is that he conduct himself with enough charm and geniality, so that he makes every situation a pleasant one by their standards. Depending on the character of the occasion, this may call for wittiness, for friendliness, for flowery language, or for various other types of conduct.

Thus the attributes of *simpatico* do not go deep, but that does not mean that they are a gloss which is easily acquired. To be considered *simpatico* a man's actions must be seen as both appropriate and spontaneous. If his flowery salutations seem forced and awkward he is not *simpatico*. If he is unduly deferential to subordinates, he is not *simpatico*, even though he may be trying very hard to be friendly and pleasant. The capacity to make people comfortable or at ease by conduct which fits their expectations is essential.

Back of these requirements of appropriateness and spontaneity are the characteristic attitudes of the individualistic personality and the values of the Mexican culture. Every man assumes in others a high propensity to seek personal ends by a variety of maneuvers. People are by instinct suspicious. The man whose efforts to be *simpatico* appear forced is immediately suspect. If it is not instinctive with him, if he seems to be trying too hard to do the right thing at the right moment, then the first presumption is that he is making a deliberate effort to make an impression to gain some personal advantage. Conduct of this character is definitely *antipatico*.

The typical United States executive will therefore find that it is not easy to become *simpatico*. Some men have within their natures the type of personal charm and social instinct which makes them without effort *simpatico* (or its equivalent) in any society. But many United States executives do not have such personalities. They may have a friendly manner, but their sense of what is appropriate to a given situation is instinctively governed by the social customs of the United States, not the local culture. Thus their efforts to be pleasant are often awkward and incorrect in the eyes of foreigners. They have to make a conscious effort to observe and practice the forms of action and speech which compose the local custom. In the course of making this effort they are likely to make blunders and to arouse the suspicions of people who see in their inept efforts sinister schemes for personal advantage, or perhaps a condescending attitude toward local ways which hurts their pride. Because of these problems, United States executives are sometimes better advised to stick to their own instinctive patterns of conduct, so they will at least appear reasonably natural and consistent. In general, however, the effort to adopt local customs does seem desirable and feasible. The difficulty of the task must be appreciated, however, and, if the goal is to be regarded as *simpatico*, the executive requires patience and persistence in his effort.

Sencillo

Another word, *sencillo*, cropped up frequently in this research as descriptive of United States executives who were liked by their Mexican associates. *Sencillo* is defined by the dictionary as "simple; easy; plain; unadorned; unaffected." Again the last definitions are the closest to the common usage. They do not, however, give a very meaningful picture. The Mexican executives who used the term felt that its meaning could not be conveyed in a handful of words. To them it describes a contrast in relationships which can only be understood as part of their culture.

Sencillo describes the opposite of certain personal qualities of authoritarian superiors which the subordinate does not like. In Mexico there is a long tradition of harsh, domineering superiors who assume airs of importance and require humiliating obeisance from subordinates. The cultural standards tolerate these qualities. The man who has them often commands great formal respect and power. Subordinates are accustomed to this type of man whether he be a father, a teacher, or a boss. They accept the humiliation and discomfort which their upward relations involve as part of life, and usually compensate for it by dominating their own subordinates. But accepting is not the same as liking, and that is why the *sencillo* executive is so appreciated. With him the Mexican can feel at ease and important.

This is the background of the word *sencillo*. Defining it is complicated because the important element in its meaning is the feeling of the particular Mexican executive using it and not any objectively measurable quality in the superior. We may, however, observe a few characteristics common to most executives who are considered *sencillo*. They are not overly concerned about building up their own importance, especially not at the expense of subordinates. They are direct in their dealings with subordinates so the latter know what is expected of them and do not blunder or get tricked into embarrassing errors. They give instructions and suggestions in a nice manner. They are understanding about problems which subordinates bring to them and helpful about solving them. Their manner is generally such that the subordinates feel they are readily approachable. In all of these characteristics a deep sincerity is essential. Whereas *simpatico* describes only superficial manner, *sencillo* describes a fundamental quality in a man's personality.

Being *sencillo* does not necessarily mean being democratic. The qualities run in that direction but not all the way, and it is apparent from watching men who are described as *sencillo* that a man may be relatively authoritarian and still meet this test. He may, for example, hold a large amount of authority in his own hands and expect his subordinates to bring many questions to him for decisions. If, as is not uncommon, the subordinates find this arrangement acceptable, he will be regarded as *sencillo* if he uses his authority in a courteous and direct manner. For example, when his men come to him for decisions, he will not expect them to show a subservient manner, and rather than giving curt orders he may take trouble to explain to the men the reasons for his position.

The *sencillo* attitude is in theory natural to the United States executive, but in reality it proves troublesome. The ideology of the United States culture calls for just the type of actions which the *sencillo* executive should follow. And in practice many executives show a large portion of these qualities. In other cases, however, United States executives depart notably from the United States ideology. Many people have noted the difference between the actions of United States citizens at home and abroad. For example, the Useems report the observations of several Indians:

> It is easier to get along with Americans in America than in India. In America there is little chance to show off, for everybody has so much; here the Americans show off. Here they tend to look down on Indians. Americans lose much of their humility—they start feeling intellectually superior. Americans are more authoritarian than in America. . . . Here the Americans are clannish, they restrict themselves to their own group. Americans at home are hospitable but here [in India] they do not ask you to their house; they remain more to themselves. . . . The foreigners in India differ from those in their own country. At first when they come they are sympathetic to Indians but in time they become anti-Indian. They forget their modesty and their notions of equality when they come here.[18]

These generalizations do not apply to all United States executives abroad, of course, but they apply to enough so that the problem assumes significant proportions. Exactly what happens to those who do fit this pattern is hard to say. Probably many left the United States because they did not like its culture. Their conduct abroad may therefore be a true expression of their personalities which, while in the United States, were forced into a degree of conformity to our ideology by social pressures. A study by Perlmutter suggests that many of those who are anxious to go abroad are misfits of this sort.[19] But many of

---

[18] John Useem and Ruth Hill Useem, "Images of the United States and Britain Held by Foreign-educated Indians," *The Annals* (Philadelphia: The American Academy of Political and Social Science), September, 1954, p. 78.
[19] Howard V. Perlmutter, "Some Characteristics of the Xenophilic Personality," *The Journal of Psychology*, 1954, 38, pp. 291–300.

the men whose ways offend the foreigners were at home rather average people. While this research did not probe far into their experience, some general observations confirmed by other studies indicate that these people suffer from significant adjustment problems in the foreign environment.[20] As they seek a satisfactory pattern for life they are likely to take two courses, both of which run counter to the requisites of being *sencillo*.

First, they tend to protect themselves from the discomforts and challenges presented by the new environment; to seek escape from the strains of culture shock. Physically this usually results in associating with other United States executives and limiting contacts with foreigners to the essential minimum. Intellectually and emotionally it means the affirmation of faith in United States superiority in all phases of life from management methods to religion. To the foreigner a United States executive following this course appears as a distant, cold individual absorbed with building himself up at the expense of the local executives.

The second pitfall is the inept drifting into authoritarian patterns of action which was mentioned in the last chapter. It is possible to be authoritarian and *sencillo*, but it is not easy for the United States executive who is used to democratic patterns. For example, in a democratic structure subordinates may accept a good deal of frank criticism from above because they know they are free to answer back if they feel the criticism is unjustified. But in an authoritarian structure the subordinate does not feel that freedom. Lacking an effective check on his actions, the United States executive may drift into a pattern similar to that of the harsh authoritarian disliked by the foreign executive.

On the whole the men who were not considered *sencillo* in their relations had made unsatisfactory adjustments in both of these respects. By contrast the *sencillo* executives had integrated their business and social lives with the native society and had made a sensitive adjustment to the patterns of interpersonal relations to which their subordinates were accustomed. That is, some of them were relatively authoritarian but carried it off in a manner which their subordinates appreciated, while others were relatively democratic.

[20] Mottram Torre, "Personality Adjustment in Overseas Service," *The Art of Overseasmanship*, edited by Harlan Cleveland and Gerard J. Mangone (Syracuse, N.Y.: Syracuse University Press, 1957), pp. 83-93.

Personalized Relations

"If you're going to work with Mexicans, you need to have a personal touch. You have to have men come down here who can appreciate people and make them feel at home." These words of one Mexican executive are typical of the attitudes of men observed in this study. They are part of the general cultural concepts of personalism which researchers find common throughout Latin America.[21] They contrast with the impersonal approach to much of life which characterizes the United States culture; an approach which leads to such observations as, "Let's keep personalities out of this," or, "I don't want to put this on a personal basis." In the Latin American culture the personal element is inescapable. One cannot avoid it. The problem is rather how to make the best use of it.

Personalized, rather than impersonal relations with the boss, are generally desired by Mexican executives. Just how personalized and in what way is a tricky question, however. As the discussion of *simpatico* suggested, there are limits to the intrusion into his personal life which the Mexican will tolerate.

From observing satisfactory relationships in this research, it appeared that a pattern such as the following met with general approval though, of course, there were notable variations. The superior showed a regular interest in the physical welfare of the subordinate and his family. He frequently demonstrated individually-directed feelings by such means as remembering the man's saint's day, and calling him by the affectionate diminutive (Juanito, etc.). He took a personal hand in helping the man in a variety of ways, in one case, for example, arranging a change in a man's work schedule so he could go to a late afternoon university course. When the subordinate brought problems to him, the superior would talk about them and give advice if he felt certain it was sound. About here, however, came the border line. He did not attempt to lead the discussion into an exposure of the subordinate's thinking and feelings, even where these were obviously fundamental to the problem. The subordinate for his part preferred to keep his basic philosophy and a large part of his affairs to himself.

Out of this relationship the Mexican derived a feeling that the

[21] William F. Whyte and Allan R. Holmberg, "Human Problems of U.S. Enterprise in Latin America," *Human Organization*, Fall, 1956, p. 3.

superior knew he was there and would take a responsibility for his welfare. He did not, however, feel that he had lost the control over his destiny which the privacy of his basic thinking provided. This last element must be understood because it is sharply opposed to much in modern United States culture, ranging from the soap opera to the career counselor. A philosophy has risen in the United States that it is good for people to share their inner thoughts and problems for the sake of therapeutic benefits and because the advice of others may be helpful. I don't propose to analyze the soundness of that philosophy but simply to emphasize that it is not incorporated in the traditional Mexican requisites of a personalized relationship. Once the individual shares his basic thinking with another, he loses tactical advantages. The superior will know his weaknesses, his hopes and other aspects of his thinking, and in maneuvering relationships these may be used against him. The strength of the individualistic personality in the struggle of life lies in the maintenance of an effective facade and not in the exposure of his inner character. The importance of this personal privacy to the Mexican is emphasized by Octavio Paz in his analysis of Mexican character:

> The popular language reflects the idea of defending ourselves against the outside: the idea of "manliness" consists in never "opening ourselves." Those that "open" themselves are cowards. For ourselves, contrary to what occurs with other people, to open oneself is a weakness or treachery. The Mexican can give in, humiliate himself, lower himself, but never open himself; that is, allow the outside world to penetrate his intimate being. The one who is opened is little to be trusted, a traitor or a man of doubtful fidelity, who tells secrets and is incapable of facing dangers as he ought. . . .
> The completely closed nature is a source of our suspiciousness and lack of confidence. It shows that instinctively we consider the environment that surrounds us perilous. This reaction is justified if one considers the history we have had and the character of the society we have created. The harshness and hostility of the atmosphere—that threat, hidden and indefinable, that is always in the air—compel us to close ourselves to the outside, like those plants of the mesa that store their juices within a spiny shell. But this conduct, legitimate in its origin, has converted itself into a mechanism that functions alone, automatically. In front of sympathy and gentleness, our recourse is reserve, because we do not know whether these sentiments are real or simulated. And furthermore, our masculine integrity is as much ashamed before

kindness as before hostility. Every opening of our inner being is an abdication of our manliness.

Our relationships with other men are also tinged with suspicion. Each time that the Mexican confides in a friend or an ,acquaintance, each time that he "opens himself," he abdicates. And he fears that the contempt of his confidant may follow his surrender. For this reason, the confidence dishonors and is as dangerous for him who makes it as for him who listens to it; unike Narcissus, we do not drown in the spring that reflects us, but we do stop it up. Our anger feeds no more on the fear of being used by our confidants—a general fear of all men—than on the shame of having renounced our solitude. He who confides, dispossesses himself. "I have sold myself to so-and-so," we say when we confide in another who doesn't deserve it. That is, we have "opened up," someone has penetrated the strong castle. The distance between man and man, created of mutual respect and mutual security, has disappeared. Not only are we at the mercy of the outsider, but also we have abdicated.[22]

On the whole, this is the basic philosophy of most Mexican executives, and it sets clear limits on the extent of personalized relationships. What they seek is the structural security of the paternalistic system, not the pervasive personal interaction desired by members of a group-oriented society.

While it is not strictly a matter of individual relationships, the organizational attitudes of foreign executives should be brought in at this point because they complement the feelings involved in the personalized relationships. Organizational feelings play an important part in the attitudes of many foreign executives. In their societies relatively small organizational units are typically unified and powerful: notably, the family, the village, and special groups such as the racial communities in India. In Chapter Two, we saw that within these units the individual may feel antagonism toward other members and he may jockey competitively against them. That does not mean, however, that he is dissatisfied with the unit itself. To the contrary, he is usually thoroughly loyal to it. The unit as a whole provides him with protection and strength and he willingly gives it his loyalty and contributes to it when his help is needed. Brother helps brother, the family pitches in to support a weak member, and so on.

---

[22] Octavio Paz, *El Laberinto de la Soledad* (México: Ediciones Cuadernos Americanos, 1950), pp. 29–30.

In Mexico, these attitudes are strong. Urbanization and other forces have weakened ties a little but the family groups are still largely intact, commanding full loyalty of members. Thus, organizational feelings are ingrained in men as they grow up and they carry them over into their working situations, looking for organizational security from the company and giving loyalty in return.

Specifically the executive expects the company to promote his personal welfare and respect his individual dignity. While a number of company policies may bear on these expectations, one group dominates the picture, namely the policies on the handling of foreign executives mentioned on page 57. The question of promotion of foreign executives is the crucial test both of the interest of the company in the individual's welfare and its respect for his dignity. No words can describe the strength of the emotions the author observed toward companies who did and did not discriminate against foreign executives in promotions. Where the foreign executive could see that the companies were really intent on giving them every opportunity to advance, they usually showed tremendous loyalty and affection for the organization. Problems of pay, pensions, and so forth command less attention but they round out the picture and in some cases appeared as a strong factor in men's feelings.

These observations, along with those about personalized relationships, combine into a picture of a desirable work atmosphere in which the individual executive feels a sense of independence and self-respect, but with security about the basic elements of his welfare. While the demands of individual foreign executives will vary greatly, a milieu of this general nature seems to be widely sought.

SUMMARY

In the first part of this chapter a number of problems were discussed which frequently contribute to undesirable attitudes in the feelings of foreign executives toward United States executives. Cultural differences, national sensitivities, anti-United States attitudes and the policies of United States companies in employment of foreign executives combine into a Pandora's box of potentially dangerous feelings which, in the absence of other forces, can plague the relations of United States executives.

The second part of the chapter dealt with the ways in which United

States executives can counteract these feelings. Recognizing the causes of the negative feelings as basically unchangeable so far as the individual is concerned, the objective has been to create conditions in which they are circumvented and submerged. The United States executive tries to build a personal relationship in which his foreign associate will feel comfortable, secure and satisfied. This effort calls for attention to the manner in which communication takes place between them, the problem of direct versus indirect communication. It requires an appreciation of the role which the foreign executive finds most acceptable in the United States executive, along the lines of the attitudes behind such words as *simpatico* and *sencillo*. Finally, there is a need to supply those personal and organizational actions which will make the individual feel his personal objectives can be met through his association with the company and the executives with whom he works.

Chapter 7

Some Broader Implications

The focus of this book has been on the individual United States executive in his efforts to build effective working relations with his foreign associates. The initial assumption was that the executive must have an understanding of the attitudes which affect the foreign executives in their work, especially those attitudes which are dominant in the culture of the country. Pursuing this assumption we have looked at the attitudes of executives toward relations with other people, their approaches to various phases of their individual work, and their motivations. We have also considered the problems and possibilities of changes in their attitudes. Finally, the special problems of relations between executives from different countries have been discussed.

To attempt at this point to summarize the material in the book does not seem sensible. What the individual executive may learn from this analysis can only be gained as he draws wisdom and understanding from thinking through the detailed discussion and cases.

On the other hand, a different form of summary does seem in order. While the book has been written for the individual executive, in many instances it has been evident that the findings of the study have implications for general management policy. These implications have not been systematically pursued so it is not possible to deal with them thoroughly. They can, however, be outlined briefly both as suggestions of subjects which managements might profitably explore, and as directions in which further research may be considered. While there are quite a range of such implications, three areas seem to me most significant.

It is amply demonstrated by this study that special administrative problems confront the United States executive in a foreign assignment. While each man, by his own effort, may hope to advance his competence in dealing with these problems, the management of a company can do other things to improve the effectiveness of the executives it sends abroad. All companies make some efforts in this direction and many do a great deal. Observing these varied efforts and their results in the field, I would suggest three subjects as those requiring the greatest attention.

First, the quality of the men sent abroad needs to be constantly upgraded. This implies, of course, careful selection but more important it requires giving greater attention to the attractiveness of foreign assignments. Most especially, young men must be able to see a period of foreign work as a real opportunity for significant activity which will contribute to a fruitful career. It is apparent both in the experience of actual executives and in the worries of current college graduates that too often in the past foreign work has shut a man off from the rate of advancement he might have expected in domestic work. Many managements are currently aware of this problem and are seeking solutions to it, but much effort will be needed before it is resolved in a manner which is consistent with the needs of continuing effective management of foreign operations.

Second, with a few notable exceptions, managements have barely scratched the surface of the problem of training men for foreign work. From this study, we can see the variety of aspects of foreign cultural attitudes which men must grasp to work well with foreign executives. And this study has not even touched on such other subjects as the understanding of foreign government bureaucracies or knowledge of foreign legal systems which are also important for effective work abroad. A great many senior executives are conscious of these needs but, other than sending men to language courses, most of them leave their education to an individual, haphazard process to be accomplished in spare time. There are, to be sure, obstacles in the uncertainty of assignments, the speed with which men are often dispatched abroad, and the costs of training. But the need being so evident, further exploration of possible training methods seems necessary.

Third, the continuing development of the skills of United States executives in their relations with foreign executives should receive greater attention. Evaluation procedures and development programs are now established in most companies, but only a very few of them give special attention to the unique problems of foreign work. One of the simplest steps which might be taken is to introduce into executive evaluation forms items such as: "How well does this man adjust to the local attitudes?" and, "To what extent has he integrated with the local society?" Just a very few companies have adopted this idea but it offers great promise as a psychological device. It serves to alert men at all levels of management that a conscious effort to adapt is important and will be rewarded. So far as development programs are concerned, we need to explore further the methods management could employ to help the executive in his efforts to learn about and adjust to the local culture. Other than a few orientation programs usually offered by bi-national cultural institutes abroad, there is relatively little effort in this direction.

POLICIES FOR FOREIGN EXECUTIVES

Virtually all companies now accept as sound policy that they should use foreign executives extensively to manage their foreign units. There remain, however, a variety of problems in accomplishing this objective in a manner consistent with optimum operating efficiency. Two of these problems may be singled out as most critical.

First, managements need to give more thought to the administrative training of foreign executives. For the most part, current efforts are directed at developing management skills by much the same formulae as are employed for similar United States executives. Without questioning the merits of these programs which appear generally valuable, I suggest that the problems evident in the attitudes revealed in this study require a further training effort. A few companies have adopted that view. One company, for example, looking to the day when a now fairly young executive will hold a senior position, plans to bring him to the United States for as much as a year. By making him an operating part of the home office and having him live in an American family, they hope he will become thoroughly conversant with American attitudes. When he returns home he may then have a bi-cultural orientation and can serve as an effective bridge between his own society and the company. This particular formula may be neither feasible nor effective in other cases. It is, however, an attack on a problem to which we should direct more attention.

Second, there is the question of whether or not foreign executives should be given the senior and most critical positions, especially those of top operating executive (president or general manager) and senior financial officer (treasurer or controller), and, if they should, what types of men should be selected. The assignment of foreign executives to these positions has significant implications for leadership and the maintenance of high standards of administrative efficiency in foreign units. In Chapter Five I mentioned the difficulties which confront a native of a country in enforcing standards which are counter to those of the local culture and the rarity of foreign executives who could perform such a task. Because it is not easy to determine whether a man has this capacity, a company faces the possibility that the transfer of senior positions to foreign executives will result in a change in administrative patterns in the direction of the local culture. It is not impossible that the new approach may be more effective than the imperfect adjustments of United States executives to local conditions and attitudes. These consequences must, however, be comprehended as a quite different order of problem from those involved in turning over lower echelon jobs to foreign executives.

The question of placing foreign executives in senior posts is one which companies will be facing with increasing frequency in coming years. It would be well at this relatively early stage to examine the problem thoroughly, particularly the experience in those cases where the step has already been taken, to determine the full character of the question and the ways in which it can be handled.

HOME OFFICE RELATIONS WITH FOREIGN UNITS

Finally, there is the problem of home office relations with foreign units which are fully staffed with foreign executives, including licensees and distributors as well as subsidiaries. We have observed a variety of impediments to communication between United States and foreign executives. For men working together with frequent daily contact, overcoming these obstacles may appear difficult. They are scarcely comparable, however, with the difficulties where most communication is by mail, with brief and infrequent personal contact, as is typically the case in home office-foreign unit relations. To minimize the problems companies are evolving various methods of communication, but the techniques are as yet in the experimental stage. We find, for example, men with titles like stockholder's representative, technical adviser, and liaison officer who spend all or a substantial part of their time with a foreign unit. It will require much time and thought to evolve effective patterns of responsibility and conduct for these men. Likewise, there are notable variations in the supervision practices of senior home office executives in their relations with their foreign associates which suggest that we still have much to learn about their proper role and the ways it may be best performed.

THE CHALLENGE AHEAD

These observations about management policies underscore one basic point, that differences in cultural attitudes between United States and foreign executives are a concern of both the individual executive and management as a whole. We can expect, given a modicum of world peace, that in coming years the interests of United States business abroad will grow far beyond their already large proportions. This prospect is enticing in the potential economic rewards it offers and hopeful in the contributions United States industry may make to the progress of other lands. It assures, however, a persisting challenge to the perception and flexibility of a great variety of individual executives and company organizations. In closing I can but express a heartfelt hope that this challenge will be met squarely and successfully both in the interests of effective operating results and the furtherance of good will among the peoples and nations of the world.

Research and Conceptual Plan

This appendix is provided for those who may wish a fuller picture of the research and thinking which lie behind this book.

RESEARCH

The material for this study was derived from several types of research. The main field work was conducted during 1955 and 1957. In the first phase the home offices and Mexican units of twenty-two United States companies were visited and forty-five United States and six Mexican executives were interviewed. Each man was visited only once, the interviews ranging from a few minutes to two hours but usually about an hour. The interviews were informal but quite directive, the men being asked specifically what problems they observed in relations between United States and foreign executives and what factors tended to lessen these problems. Out of this survey of opinions the basic cultural hypothesis of the research evolved and around it a number of subsidiary hypotheses.

The second phase was designed to test these hypotheses through analysis of specific administrative situations. The preliminary survey had indicated certain management groups whose relationships seemed reasonably representative. Within these groups six United States and ten Mexican executives were observed and interviewed intensively over a four-month period. The men were watched in group meetings and individual interactions and a number of essentially non-directive interviews were held with each. The contacts with the men were full enough so that a high degree of confidence and consequent free discussion with the interviewer developed. This research provided a detailed picture of the personality characteristics and behavior patterns of the men and their effects in the conduct of the administrative process of the organizations.

Supporting the field research was extensive exploration of the environment of foreign administrative situations. A number of social scientists and other people acquainted with foreign relationships were interviewed, and the literature describing cultural attitudes and intercultural problems was studied. In sum, this exploration provided the setting against which the executive relationship problems could be analyzed.

Finally, while not part of the planned research, it must be noted that the author had been personally involved in administrative relationships over a number of years with many foreign nationals: Turks, Mexicans, Indians, Frenchmen, and others. It is doubtful if the observations derived from the research would have been as meaningful without this degree of personal awareness of the emotions and attitudes present in intercultural relations.

THE CONCEPTUAL FRAMEWORK

The thesis of cultural differences which developed out of this research has been outlined in Chapter One. Attendant to that thesis are several conceptual considerations. It did not seem desirable to interrupt the flow of the basic study by presenting them in the body of the book but they are included here to answer questions which might arise in the readers' minds about the point of view adopted by the author.

Culture and Personality

In adopting the cultural orientation this study immediately encountered the question of the relation between the culture of a group and the attitudes of an individual executive. To clarify this relationship, a few fundamental concepts about a culture and its significance in the lives of men and nations must be established.

The culture of a group is broadly defined as an integrated pattern of beliefs on the basis of which men learn to live with their environment. It includes beliefs about nature and the supernatural, attitudes about how men should treat each other, codes of morals, and all the other fundamentals which govern men's lives and give them a measure of peace and mental security. In a sense the cultural pattern provides a set of guiding principles from which men can draw answers to the problems of life. Each individual has attitudes of the same general character which are part of his personality and his attitudes are related to the culture of his group. The nature of the relationship is often confused, however.

The most important point is a negative one. The attitudes of all members of a group are not identical with the culture of the group as a whole. Each individual is the product of a unique combination of inner personal qualities and environmental conditions. Thus, when we describe the culture of a group such as the middle- and upper-class, urban Mexicans, we are not describing personality characteristics common to all Mexicans in those classes. This distinction is important when speaking about business executives, because their attitudes may depart considerably from the group culture.

For example, a general characteristic of the Mexican culture is the authoritarian attitude of men in superior positions. Yet several Mexican executives were observed in this study who were distinctly democratic in their handling of subordinates. Similar variations are found among United States executives. In the United States culture such relationships are governed by democratic principles, but the actions of some United States executives observed in Mexico indicated strong authoritarian tendencies.

The culture of a group cannot, therefore, be taken as a statement of the characteristics which will be found in each member of the group. Its relation to the personality patterns of the members lies rather in two mutually supporting aspects: (1) it describes frequently found characteristics; and (2) it forms the ideology of the group.

In combination these two points explain the existence of the group culture. Each component of the culture represents an adjustment which most of the people have found satisfactory in meeting a situation in their common environment. These common attitudes have then become a part of the ideology of the group, providing the continuity and stability that all groups need for effectiveness. Once a belief becomes part of the ideology of the group it is then passed on to new generations by the family, the church, the schools and other social institutions. Thus most children will grow up with these beliefs and their attitude will propagate the beliefs as part of the ideology.

Both the frequency and ideology aspects are significant in working with foreign executives. Knowing that some characteristic is frequently found among members of a cultural group gives the executive overseas leads as to what to look for. If Harry Grey (in Chapter One) knew that avoiding frank discussions with superiors was a Mexican cultural characteristic, he could approach his relations with Pedro Gomez more intelligently. He could not be sure at the outset that Pedro felt that way, but he would realize there was a good possibility that Pedro had thoughts about the parts problem which would be hard to bring out.

The ideology of the group affects the individual executive in two ways: first, in his feelings about himself and second, in his expectations of others. Internally the beliefs and standards of the group influence his judgments about the adequacy and correctness of his own attitudes. If these attitudes are similar to the ideology, he feels reinforced in his position. Actions and points of view which conform to the culture seem natural to him, and even when they appear inappropriate to the outsider, the executive is not likely to feel a sense of guilt about them. For example, because of the wide acceptance of the value of personalized relationships in business, Pedro felt his attitude toward keeping Ramex (or as he saw it, Carlos) as his supplier was the "right" way to do business.

The expectations with which an executive approaches his relations with others are strongly influenced by the group ideology, whether his own beliefs conform to the ideology or not. This is a practical matter. When a man lives and works with a group, he must either adjust his expectations to their standards or face constant frustration and ineffectiveness. It is just such an adjustment that we have seen the United States executive needs in his relationship with foreign executives. Here, we are dealing with the continuing adjustments which a man makes throughout life in the variety of relationships he encounters within his own society. Ideally his expectations should be specially tailored to the personality of each individual as he is encountered. In fact, because of the limitations of time and personal adaptability, a man can hope to approach this goal in only a few intimate relationships. Otherwise his adjustments tend to be in terms of stereotypes and cultural patterns. He has a set of expectations for people in general and then more definite sets for salesgirls, for subordinates and so on. Depending on how much he knows about a specific person he may modify the expectations further, but these general patterns are the starting point and to a considerable degree they are instinctive, which means that any modification requires a deliberate effort.

These general patterns of expectations are not identical with the ideology because unique elements in the individual's personality are bound to influence them. But they follow the ideology closely because many of a man's expectations are acquired from the ideology as he hears it described by people around him throughout life, and also because he finds through experience that the ideology is valid—that people do frequently act according to its codes. Therefore, expectations drawn from the ideology prove effective in dealing with life.

Thus the expectations and resultant actions of all members of a group show more similarity than the actual attitudes of the individuals. United States executives abroad and at home demonstrate this fact time and again—expecting actions of others to fall into a fairly uniform pattern, but themselves clearly differing from this pattern in some way or other. The difference between individual attitudes and ideologically derived expectations is therefore something they must understand in themselves. In addition, it is something which must be in mind in order to comprehend the actions of foreign executives who, in relations with their fellow nationals, consciously or more often unconsciously apply the group beliefs rather than their own.

For example, Manuel Durango was quite effective in working with other departments in his company. He cooperated with them readily and when disputes arose, he could work them out while still maintaining good relations. This was not true of most of his subordinates who, like Pedro Gomez, were suspicious of others and worked independently. When they had disagreements with other departments, they usually ended in arguments and bad feelings. Manuel was not pleased with this situation, but he was uncritical of the subordinates. "That's the way they are. I can't expect them to be able to work well with those fellows. It's just in their natures to fight that way."

The frequency with which cultural attitudes are found among foreign executives and the effect which their ideological acceptance has on the feelings and expectations of the executives explain their significance in analyzing the attitudes of individual men. One further concept is necessary, however, to put the meaning of culture in proper perspective.

Cultures are not static. The frequent occurrence of each cultural attitude and its ideological support provide powerful forces for its propagation. But in spite of all, cultures change. They change for a reason which is implicit in our initial definition. Each attitude represents a way of adjusting to the environment of the group. Changes come as the environment changes.

In working with foreign executives this perspective is clearly important. Environments are changing rapidly in the underdeveloped countries which are industrializing at a fast pace and even in the European countries in which established industrial practices are being uprooted. Furthermore, in most countries of the world significant political and social changes have been underway in recent years. Mexico provides a striking, but by no means unusual, case in point. The Mexican environment and culture remained virtually constant from the Spanish conquest till around 1910. Since then the country has been going through a period of rapid transition. The political system has moved steadily toward greater democracy and less corruption; the secular power of the church has been shattered and the church is rebuilding its position on a new basis; family ties have loosened; industrialization and urbanization have proceeded rapidly; and a powerful labor movement has been organized—to mention just the most striking developments.

Considering these profound changes the Mexican culture has shown amazing persistence. It seems likely that the forces for the propagation of a culture have preserved many attitudes into a time when they are not really applicable to the environment. Approaching the problem from another direction, a Mexican psychiatrist makes such an observation after studying the attitudes of a sample of the Mexico City population:

> Those socio-cultural norms are probably the most rigidly implanted in the Mexican environment. Mexicans frequently consider such values as basic and as almost natural characteristics, basic constituents of the Mexican nationality. Frequently one hears that the Mexican way ought to remain constant and it is not unusual that any attempt at change in such spheres is considered as a betrayal of the people of Mexico. . . .

From the point of view of mental hygiene it would be advisable to discuss these points more deeply. Mexico has changed profoundly with the Mexican Revolution and with recent industrialization, and it is very probably inadequate to maintain norms that no longer reflect the reality of present day Mexico. Traditions, like old maps, may well no longer represent in their framework the new territories and naturally lead to frustration and conflict and therefore to unhappiness and mental illness.[1]

The culture of a group should not be regarded therefore as rigid. More likely it will be changing slowly, probably more slowly than the environment justifies and the well-being of its members requires, but nevertheless changing. I have already noted that the attitudes of foreign executives will often not conform to those of their cultural group. While this may be due to chance deviations, it frequently appears that they have made a more realistic adjustment to their environment than their group. These executives seem to be the advance guard in the general process of cultural change. Their attitudes will probably be those which are commonly accepted in later generations.

For the United States executive abroad this process of cultural change is of great importance. It means in the first place that complete conformance to the existing culture is neither necessary nor desirable. His task is rather to observe the ways in which change is coming and to work with the process, neither pressing it too hard nor blocking its progress. In more practical terms, it means, as Dr. Diaz indicates, that his associates have problems of adjustment with which he may be able to help. Some may be holding to beliefs which do not fit their situations and lead to the frustrations which in the extreme concern the psychiatrist. Others may be out ahead of their group seeking new attitudes which do fit the environment and looking for support and understanding in their inevitably lonely position.

This perspective also has importance in the oft-debated question of "imposing United States methods on foreign peoples." The whole question is too big to be explored here. There is, however, one aspect which is pertinent to this discussion. The problems of life in a dynamic, highly industrialized urban society are not identical in all countries, but they are similar. The United States has virtually completed the transition to such a society in the past century. Our cul-

---

[1] Rogelio Diaz-Guerero, "Teoria y Resultados Preliminares de un Ensayo de Determinacion del Grado de Salud Mental, Personal y Social del Méxicano de la Ciudad," *Psiquis*, 2:31, 1952, p. 32.

ture has changed greatly in that time and now reflects, however imperfectly, an adjustment to our industrial environment.

Currently vast areas of the world are in the early stages of similar transitions. They started from somewhat different points and the form their societies will ultimately achieve will probably differ also. Thus the transitions will not be the same as that of the United States. But surely there is much which can be learned from the United States experience which can be applied in easing the transitions of other cultures.

Coverage of Cultures

The greater part of this book is devoted to discussing Mexican administrative situations with only occasional mention of other cultures. It is presented, however, as a study valuable for United States executives in any culture. This approach was adopted with several considerations in mind.

In the first place there are practical reasons for avoiding a study comprehensive of all important cultures. There are over fifty countries in which United States companies have significant business interests. The culture of each is distinctive in some respects. Furthermore, there are important differences in culture among regions, classes and other groupings in most countries. Short of writing an encyclopedia, it is obviously impossible to describe all, or even an appreciable portion of, the specific cultural differences which United States executives may meet overseas. This is just as well. Armed with such a specific book, the unwary executive might be led into assuming that he had a precise handbook to understanding each foreign executive he met. In view of the tremendous range of individuals found even within a supposedly unified cultural group, this would be a dangerous deception.

Beyond this essentially negative position, however, is a positive argument for concentration in the main on one culture. The objective of this book is not to give information but rather to present a way of thinking. The heart of it lies in the methodology, the pattern of analysis of a culture and its impact on administrative attitudes. A thorough and comprehensive grasp of the character of the culture is essential. With this orientation, concentration on one country becomes inevitable. Jumping from country to country hitting high spots or attempting to sum up national characters in a few pages misses the point completely, and an attempt at thorough analysis of several cultures at the same time would exhaust both writer and reader. Thus Mexico was taken as a case upon which the methodology is tested and illustrated. Mexico is representative of other countries in many respects, so that it provides a good testing ground. What emerged from the study, therefore, is a picture of a basic approach to understanding the attitudes of foreign executives made meaningful by its thorough application to a specific culture.

This is sufficient reason for limiting the main analysis to one culture. It has, however, seemed wise to include references to other cultures from time to time. This, in part, is a check against the possible inference that a characteristic observed in Mexico is universally true in other cultures. The range of attitudes present in Mexico gives some check of this sort but in many cases the point is made more forcefully by reference to other cultures where the differences are more common and strong. In addition, observations are sometimes made about other cultures to provide a degree of confirming breadth on points which are notable for their world-wide prevalence. The reader is justified in asking from time to time, "This seems to be true of Mexico but I wonder how it applies elsewhere." and, within the limits of reasonable space, answers have been supplied frequently.

Thus, in sum, the book presents a broadly applicable methodology, a penetrating application of the methodology in one culture and spot checks of it in other areas of the world.

Language and Custom

While this study has concentrated on cultural differences as the major sources of difficulties in relations between men of different nations, two aspects of culture have not been discussed, language and custom. As these aspects are very important, their deliberate omission requires explanation.

People usually observe that an executive cannot be effective in a foreign country until he learns the local language and customs. This is true, but stated in that way it does not tell the full story, because there is considerable misunderstanding about what "learning the local language and customs" means. Two levels of learning are possible, one involving mechanical acquisition of knowledge and the other requiring the development of understanding. Each has its value, but the differences between them are significant.

The first level is a literal translation process, the United States executive learning to substitute approximate foreign equivalents for United States words, phrases, mannerisms, and so forth. This degree of learning is not absolutely essential abroad, but it is helpful. On the language side, the United States executive will usually find that his immediate associates speak English so that the minimum essentials of business can be conducted in English. However, if he hopes to have real contact with men throughout his organization and in broader business, government and social circles, the executive must learn the native tongue. Furthermore, among English-speaking associates he will be more highly regarded if he makes an effort to speak to them in their own language.

Likewise, in the cosmopolitan business world an executive can get by without much concern for local custom. It helps a great deal, though, in putting foreign executives at ease and avoiding possible offenses to know the local customs; to know, for example, that in Mexico you always greet friends with a firm handshake or a hearty *abrazo* (embrace), while in India such physical contact is generally avoided.

The second level of learning, and to some people it is the only true learning, is the understanding of foreign language and custom as part of the personality patterns and total culture of the country. The substitution processes used in the first type of learning are to some degree a deception. They imply a uniformity of situations with only mechanical differences in the words or actions which people apply in them. One is led to assume that "greeting friends" is a uniform event and the difference between a Mexican *abrazo* and United States handshake is simply a practical difference in the way people deal with that situation. In fact this may or may not be true and, until we know what a friend means to a Mexican or what emotions he feels when he greets him, we cannot be sure. The confusion surrounding the word *simpatico* which is discussed in Chapter Six is a good example of the errors which people can fall into in relying on literal translations without grasping the feelings which lie behind words.

The reason for avoiding specific discussion of language and custom in this book is to direct full attention at the type of understanding which this second level of learning requires. I hope this will help to redress a current unbalance in favor of the first level. The emphasis of linguists and anthropologists on learning language and customs has been widely interpreted among the general populace as meaning the acquisition of specific foreign words, practices, and so forth, according to the mechanical process all too common in our schools. This is unfortunate because most of the experts are fundamentally interested in the second level. But it is a fact and, to one observing foreign executives abroad, it is clear that many of them approach their learning with this limited type of objective in mind.

By and large, they are convinced of the value of learning language and customs, but relatively few of them see this task as related to understanding foreign personalities—a subject which is treated as a separate matter. It would have been possible in this book to try to argue for a different approach by elaborating further on the relation of these elements of learning. I have not undertaken that, however, because it seems to me that the important objective is helping to the utmost the United States executive in his efforts to understand foreign personalities. As this understanding advances, the deeper level of language and custom learning will come naturally.

The Individual and the Group

This appendix is a brief explanation of the differences between two concepts of the relations of individuals and groups which have been noted in several places in this book. Because of the limitations of our language, the words used to describe these concepts are quite similar, yet they concern distinctly different attitudes. Briefly the distinction may be stated thus:

(1) *Individualistic* versus *Group-oriented* describes a contrast in attitudes toward people with whom the individual has immediate contact and under conditions in which he has a sense of personal control over his actions.

(2) *Individualism* versus *Group-submission* describes a contrast in the attitudes of the individual toward his position in relation to his society and environment.

The first concept is thoroughly elaborated in Chapter Two, so it need not be expanded here, other than to emphasize that it applies only to the attitudes which influence the way a man acts in those situations where the codes of his society give him freedom in determining the types of relationships he develops with people and groups around him.

The second concept is at a different level. The key distinction between individualism and group-submission is the sense of independence and power to change status. Where group-submission prevails the individual does not have that sense. The major elements in his life are regarded as predetermined. He does not feel he can change such things as his social status, his educational level, and his economic class. He views the character of the world around him as relatively fixed and his own position in it as beyond his control. Furthermore, in daily life he recognizes the authority of groups like the family, the church, and the ruling hierarchy. Obedience and loyalty to the codes established by these institutionalized groups are not fundamentally questioned.

Individualism is associated with the concepts of liberalism and self-determination. The essential tenet is the feeling of the individual that he is free to determine his own destiny and has the power to modify substantially both the environment and his own position in it.

These two concepts are confusing just because of the similarity in the words associated with them. But the confusion is compounded because there appears to be a relation in the appearance of these qualities in cultures with opposites in terms applying frequently to a given culture. That is, in those cultures which encourage individualism, there seems to be a greater tendency to group-orientation, and in those where group-submission is dominant, the individualistic personality is more common.

This book is no place to explore such a complex subject, but it is worth noting that this bit of semantic confusion is probably no accident. It appears that most people need a relation to a group for security and other personal satisfactions, and they also need a degree of personal liberty. In the group-submissive society, a man's association with groups is dictated, so what we see in the individualistic personality is apparently the exercise of what freedom he has in patterns of struggle and conflict within the group. The codes of individualism set the individual free from fixed groups, but they also give him freedom to seek his own groups. Not wanting complete freedom, he seems to associate himself willingly with various groups and in the process gives up much of his freedom to the groups.